THE BIBLE SAYS YOU CAN

EXPECT
THESE THINGS

CLYNE W. BUXTON

*To Brother Lowery
with best wishes.
— Clyne*

142

FLEMING H. REVELL COMPANY
OLD TAPPAN, NEW JERSEY

Unless indicated otherwise, all Scripture quotations in this volume are from the King James Version of the Bible.

Scripture quotations identified as PHILLIPS are from The New Testament in Modern English translated by J.B. Phillips, copyright J.B. Phillips, 1958. Used by permission of the Macmillan Company.

Scripture quotations identified as BERKELEY are from the Berkeley Version in Modern English and are used by permission of the publishers, Zondervan Publishing House.

Scripture quotations identified as TLB are from The Living Bible by Kenneth N. Taylor © copyright 1971, and are used by permission of the publisher, Tyndale House Publishers.

Scripture quotations identified as NEB are from The New English Bible © The Delegates of the Oxford University Press and the Syndics of the Cambridge University Press 1961 and 1970. Reprinted by permission.

Scripture quotations identified as AMPLIFIED are from The Amplified New Testament, By permission of the Lockman Foundation.

Lines from the song "His Name is Wonderful," by Audrey Mieir, are © copyright 1959 by Manna Music, Incorporated, North Hollywood, California.

Lines from the song "You Will Be My Closest Neighbor Up There," by Albert E. Brumley, are copyright 1938 by the Stamps-Baxter Music Company in "Brightest Beams." Copyright © Renewed 1966. All Rights Reserved. Used By Permission

Library of Congress Cataloging in Publication Data

Buxton, Clyne W
    The Bible says you can expect these things.

    Half title: Expect these things.
    Bibliography: p
        1. Bible—Prophecies.   I. Title.   II. Title:
    Expect these things.
    BS647.2.B8   220.1′5   72–10330
    ISBN 0–8007–0572–6

To my wife, Mary,
and my daughter, Clynette,
who share with me
a deep interest in God's word

Contents

Preface

Once we are born we are destined to live on forever, and this book concerns what we can expect to happen to us throughout our eternal future. Within these pages I have not attempted to be profound; perhaps that would have been a futile effort anyway. Rather, I have tried to write so that the layman and the common man on the street may understand what he should expect in the future. Therefore, if I have written a clear, easy-to-follow treatise on things to come, I have accomplished what I set out to do. You will have to be the judge of my success in the project.

I am indebted to speakers whom I have heard address themselves to predictive Scripture, and to numerous writers whose books I have avidly read. I have endeavored to give credit wherever necessary. Nonetheless, I am sure that much, and perhaps most, of what I have written I gleaned from other minds and in time assimilated into my own. As you know, few things are original with any of us.

I am deeply indebted to Dr. Donald N. Bowdle, professor at Lee College and editor of the new, one-volume *Ellicott's Bible Commentary*. He read the manuscript in its entirety, gave valuable assistance in correcting expressions, and suggested changes in the wording of precise, theological statements. I have the same indebtedness to the Reverend David L. Lemons, also of

Lee College, who is widely known for his thorough, analytical knowledge of the Scriptures. He, too, carefully read the entire manuscript, noting valuable suggestions to me.

Further, I must express my genuine gratitude to Miss Joyce Green, who faithfully and cheerfully labored many hours typing the manuscript and lending other valuable assistance in the preparation of it.

It is my hope that you will read this volume with your Bible close at hand, taking time to look up the nearly five hundred Biblical references which I have noted. In the back of the book you will find a listing of every scriptural reference used with page number listed. I trust this will lend assistance in the future as you return to this book seeking amplification on certain references.

May the Holy Spirit guide all of us, first into preparation for eternity and then into constant readiness, so that when life is over here we will live in the holy presence of Christ throughout our eternal future.

CLYNE W. BUXTON

1
God's Tomorrow

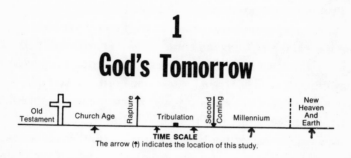

Old Testament | Church Age | Rapture | Tribulation | Second Coming | Millennium | New Heaven And Earth

TIME SCALE
The arrow (✝) indicates the location of this study.

The unparalleled truths found in the Bible concerning our incredible future stagger our imagination. When we read of the Lord Jesus snatching the believers from the world, or of a one-man, worldwide rule in the person of the Antichrist during the Tribulation, or the one-thousand-year reign of Christ right here upon this old earth—these things appear farfetched and unbelieveable to the natural mind. For you and me to expect such phenomenal happenings would qualify as extreme religious fanaticism if God's Word did not spell them out. But it does, and since we accept the Bible as God's Book we believe those things will come to pass.

Note what Jehovah Himself says about the future: "I am God, and there is none like me, Declaring the end from the beginning, and from ancient times the things that are not yet done, saying, My counsel shall stand, and I will do all my pleasure" (Isaiah 46:9,10). *Declaring the end from the beginning, and from ancient times the things that are not yet done.* What an all-wise God! And how anemic does our puny knowledge appear against the limitless knowledge of the omniscient

God, who knows all about the past, all about the present, and all about the future.

Prophecy is "heady stuff" it has been said, and we may sometimes appear sensational, though not intentionally so, when speaking of things to come. However, you will find that some of the other cardinal doctrines of the Scriptures may seem sensational, too. The virgin birth of our Lord, for example, once a part of predictive prophecy, was a phenomenal happening. Further, the very fact that the cold, lifeless body of Jesus came to life again most certainly was a supernatural event, and the thought of Christ coming again is incredible. Jehovah is a miracle-working God, and miracles, being completely out of the realm of ordinary things, are often nearly inconceivable to mortal man.

Nonetheless, God does not do things just to impress us or to be showy, and He would have you and me proceed cautiously, ". . . rightly dividing the world of truth" (2 Timothy 2:15), when delving into the future. We should speak only where the Lord speaks. John Baillie said, "The Bible indicates that the future is in God's hands. If it were in our hands, we would make a mess of it. . . ." We can also make a mess in speaking of the future if we do not stay within the Scriptures.

The Lord knows what is ahead, and He has seen fit to reveal a good deal of the future to us. He told the Apostle John, writer of the last book of the Bible, to set down three things: (1) "the things which thou hast seen"; (2) "the things which are"; (3) "the things which shall be hereafter" (Revelation 1:19).

Though John did write of what he had seen, and of the things which were, you will notice that almost all of Revelation speaks of things yet to transpire. In fact, the entire book after chapter 3 is generally considered by evangelical expositors to be futuristic.

Prophecy Overwhelms

The angel Gabriel appeared to Daniel and told him: "Behold, I will make thee know what shall be in the last end of the indignation: for at the time appointed the end shall be" (Daniel 8:19). When Daniel was shown things to come, he was overwhelmed, just as we are. Verse 27 states that he was astonished and then fainted and was sick several days!

More than 25 percent of the Bible was predictive prophecy when it was written, and to discount prophecy is to disavow over one-fourth of God's Book. The Lord Jesus fully supported prophecy, for He said: "For had ye believed Moses, ye would have believed me: for he wrote of me" (John 5:46), and John wrote ". . . the testimony of Jesus is the spirit of prophecy" (Revelation 19:10). These references point out that Christ is the center of prophecy, just as He is the center of all Scripture.

As you know, the Lord looks at the end of things from the beginning, and He can speak in His Word of the future just as easily as we can talk of history. About half of the prophetic Word is not yet fulfilled, and when one considers that we are quite probably living right at the close of this age, it is both exciting and sobering to realize that within the next few years much of prophecy could be fulfilled.

We do not have to be like Churchill, who wept as he mused on "the awful unfolding of the future," for Jesus said: "And when these things begin to come to pass, then look up, and lift up your heads; for your redemption draweth nigh" (Luke 21:-28).

Fear of Prophecy

There are several ways we can treat prophecy: (1) We can ignore it. (2) We can teach nothing else but prophecy. (3) We can teach the entire Bible, including prophecy. I am sure the last is God's way for us to deal with the future. Notwithstanding, many well-meaning people shy away from prophetic references altogether, honestly feeling that to be the best course for them.

A well-meaning friend of a minister said to him, "You had better stay out of Revelation . . . I notice those who read that book become foolish and cranky!" Speaking of prophecy in the book *God's Plan For The Future,* Lehman Strauss stated, "I believe it can be said, without fear of contradiction, that those who reject it know little or nothing about it. What a sad commentary on our church leaders, seminary leaders and pastors."

In passing over the prophetic truths concerning the future, many people may be guilty of the same error that the Jews committed when they discounted the more than three hundred predictions in their sacred writings concerning the coming of the Lord Jesus as their Messiah. Biederwolf, in the introduction of his voluminous work entitled *The Millennium Bible,* states that for twenty years he did not make one single reference in his preaching to the return of Christ.

Later he was moved to minister on the subject. Knowing that his knowledge of eschatology was almost nil, he made a thorough study of, not only the doctrine of the Second Coming of Christ, but of all eschatological references throughout the Bible. The result of his research is his 728-page book.

Prophetic Date-Setters

You are probably well aware that some people have gotten overzealous concerning the future and have gone beyond the Bible. I heard a nationally known preacher say some years ago that the Holy Spirit had revealed to him that Christ would come during that decade, but the decade passed and Christ did not return. Henry H. Halley states that he thinks some people will be disappointed if Christ does not adhere to the schedule they have made out for Him!

We know that Jesus is coming, not in man's time, but in God's time. No one knows when that time will be, not even Christ Himself. Only the Father has this knowledge. Jesus said: ". . . the exact date and hour no one knows, except the Father; neither the angels in heaven nor the Son" (Mark 13:32 BERKELEY).

Nonetheless, the Lord does reveal a great deal to us about His Son's return and the events to follow. Though He does not name the day nor the hour, "Surely the Lord God will do nothing, but he revealeth his secret unto his servants the prophets" (Amos 3:7). Just as "God . . . spake in time past unto the fathers by the prophets" (Hebrews 1:1), He still speaks to us today through the writings of those prophets.

It is a fact that wild, speculative statements concerning prophetic Scripture have caused confusion. Just before World War II and during the early years of that global conflict, some well-meaning persons tried to show that Benito Mussolini and later Adolph Hitler were the Antichrist. In fact, an entire book was written supporting the contention that Mussolini was Antichrist.

You can well understand that these and other such ill-founded speculations placed eschatology in a bad light during those days, and for years afterward a minister was thought to be neither scholarly nor tuned to the times if he preached on things to come. Those ministers who preached very much on the future were referred to as prophecy preachers, and were looked upon as being quaint and not quite all there.

Such is not the case today. I have more than eighty books in my library on eschatological themes, most of which were written within the last ten years. Lately there is definitely an accelerated interest in the future. Law, order, and morals are crumbling, and man is taking a new look into God's Word where he is finding a description of these days and what lies ahead.

An applicable Biblical reference reads:

> . . . in the last days perilous times shall come. For men shall be lovers of their own selves, covetous, boasters, proud, blasphemers, disobedient to parents, unthankful, unholy, Without natural affection, trucebreakers, false accusers, incontinent, fierce, despisers of those that are good, Traitors, heady, highminded, lovers of pleasures more than lovers of God; Having a form of godliness, but denying the power thereof: from such turn away.
> (2 Timothy 3:1–5)

As you clearly see, this is a description of contemporary world society!

Validity of the Prophet

Churchill commented, "You know I always avoid prophesying beforehand; it is much better policy to prophesy after the event has already taken place." A Greek proverb states that he who guesses best is the best prophet. Millennia ago Moses pondered this problem of a prophet's validity: "How shall we know the word which the Lord hath not spoken" (Deuteronomy 18:21)? He answers the question thus: "When a prophet speaketh in the name of the Lord, if the thing follow not, nor come to pass, that is the thing which the Lord hath not

spoken, but the prophet hath spoken it presumptuously"
(Deuteromony 18:22).

What a practical test! Old Testament prophets who foretold
the time, place, and manner of Christ's birth were bona fide
prophets because their predictions came true. Also, those stal-
warts of God who foretold His coming again were true prophets. We know He died and was resurrected. We also know that
He is coming again!

But all so-called prophets have not been genuine. An example
was William Miller, who led the great Millerite movement
(1831–1845) with such zeal and conviction that he convinced
thousands of people that Christ would return at a stated time,
which, of course, did not happen. Such erroneous preaching
makes the doctrine of things to come appear as a rash on the
otherwise clear complexion of the Church. However, such is
not really the case. Eschatology is the ruddy glow of the good
health of Christ's body, the Church.

An extra-Biblical document called the *Didache,* or the
"teaching," was written near the end of the first century. It
stated the criterion for judging an itinerant preacher. It said
that the preacher was false: (1) if he stayed more than three
nights in one home; (2) if he asked for money for himself; (3)
if he did not practice what he preached. Most of us would think
this to be a pretty good test even today!

Interpretation of Prophecy

Hermeneutics—the science of interpretation and explanation
—is of utmost importance in studying eschatology. Almost all
evangelical scholars give a literal interpretation to as much of
the Bible as possible. As David L. Cooper states in his work
When Gog's Armies Meet the Almighty in the Land of Israel:

"When the plain sense of Scripture makes common sense, seek no other sense; therefore, take every word at its primary, ordinary, usual literal meaning unless the facts of the immediate context, studied in the light of related passages and axiomatic and fundamental truths, indicate clearly otherwise."

A prophecy may have a first and partial fulfillment hundreds of years before its full and complete fulfillment. A case in point is Daniel's prediction in the ninth chapter of his book concerning the "abomination of desolation." This was partially fulfilled before Christ's birth by the desecration of the Jerusalem temple by Antiochus Epiphanes, who actually offered a pig on the altar; but it will have its final fulfillment when the Antichrist commits an abominable act in the Jewish temple during the Tribulation.

A little girl innocently asked, "If Jesus didn't mean what He said, why didn't He say what He meant?" We believe that Christ through the Holy Spirit did say what He meant, though for His own reasons He sometimes couched His statements in symbols and figures.

Purpose of Prophecy

The Bible is God's self-revelation, and it is man's only source of information concerning Jehovah's continuous, consistent account of His will revealed through numerous prophets and writers to whom the character, inner thoughts, and purpose of the Almighty God is made clear. In His Word He unfolds the great plan that was ever in His heart. A large part of His eternal plan has yet to see fruition, and that part of His plan you and I call prophecy.

Almost all prophecy relates to one of three general subjects: (1) the Gentiles; (2) the Church; (3) the Jews. Prophecy of the

Gentiles or Gentile nations is given in Daniel and Revelation, among other books. The Church, the body of Christ, is often referred to in the New Testament, and numerous references predict that the Church will be captured, or caught away to heaven. The Jews figure prominently in prophecy, and God is now returning the Jews to their ancient land in fulfillment of prophecy preparatory to fulfillment of many other Biblical prophecies about them.

Some Terms Used in Prophetic Study

Eschatology. Taken from a compound Greek word, the term is derived from *eschatos,* meaning last or latter; and *logos,* meaning discussion. Hence, eschatology is a discussion or study of last things or things to come. The word itself does not appear in the Bible.

Apocalypse. This is a name frequently given to Revelation, the last book of the Bible. It means disclosure or revelation.

Rapture. Though this word is not found in the Scriptures, its meaning so graphically depicts what will happen in the first phase of Christ's Second Coming when He comes for His own, its use is widespread. Coming from the Latin word *rapio,* which means "to snatch away suddenly," the English word *rapture,* when used in reference to Christ's return, means "to carry away to sublime happiness." The New Testament Book of Titus called the event "that blessed hope" (2:13), and so it is for you and me if we are daily serving the Lord.

The End. The Scriptures use this term often when discussing the end-times. On several occasions Jesus used it. He said, ". . . the harvest is the end of the world" (Matthew 13:39). When referring to things to come, *world* should be translated "age." Hence, the "end of the *age*" (not *world*). This is true also

in Matthew 13:40, ". . . so shall it be in the end of this world"
[Greek, *age*]. In Matthew, chapter 24, Christ referred to the
end several times. He stated, ". . . *the end* is not yet" (v. 6)
". . . and then shall the end come" (v. 14).

Last Days. This term, used repeatedly in the Scriptures, refers to the end-times. Two examples follow: ". . . in the last days
perilous times shall come" (2 Timothy 3:1), and ". . . there shall
come in the last days scoffers . . ." (2 Peter 3:3).

Other Terms. Expressions such as Antichrist, Tribulation,
Armageddon, Second Coming of Christ, Millennium, and
many others, will be defined later as they are discussed.

2

A Trip Through Space

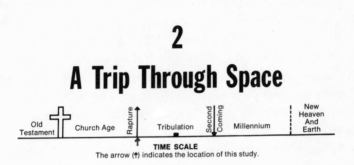

TIME SCALE
The arrow (↑) indicates the location of this study.

Millions of us were glued to our television sets on Monday morning, July 26, 1971, when at 9:34 A.M. three astronauts blasted off from Cape Kennedy. As they sped toward the moon, newsmen, searching for comparisons, made the incredible statement that the energy expended to lift the gigantic ship from the launching pad equaled the power of all streams and rivers of our nation, if harnessed. With bated breath we saw the prodigious spaceship slowly lift from the earth, then gain ever-increasing speed and quickly streak out of sight. What a technological achievement that was for science, and what an exhilarating experience for those astronauts as they raced to the moon.

Man's astounding venture into space, however, is weak in comparison to the phenomenal space trip you and I will take when Jesus comes, provided we belong to Him. Naming that epoch-making event the Rapture, or the translation of the Church, many of us today eagerly anticipate the return of Christ, which could take place at any moment. His coming will be secret and unannounced, and we who are His followers will be whisked away forever to be with the Lord (1 Thessalonians 4:17).

19

Though you and I get excited about this truth, it must surely sound preposterous to people who hear it for the first time. Yet, that notable book, the Bible, clearly, emphatically teaches the doctrine of the Rapture. It states: "Take notice; I am telling you a secret. We shall not all fall asleep but we shall all be changed, in a moment, in the twinkling of an eye, at the last trumpet call. For the trumpet shall peal and the dead shall be raised imperishably, and we shall be changed" (1 Corinthians 15:51, 52, BERKELEY).

There will be thousands upon thousands of people who will never die, and if you and I are living for Jesus, when He returns, we will be among those thousands. We will take a plain air trip through the sky, past the moon, the stars, the sun, and into heaven. The Bible speaks of how quickly we will be changed: ". . . in a moment, in the twinkling of an eye . . ." (1 Corinthians 15:52).

We will be changed suddenly, as quickly as you blink your eye, and you do that in one one-thousandth of a second! Little wonder that Christ likens His coming to that of a thief who slips in quickly, and quietly carts off valuables from a home. The Lord will return and secretly sweep us from this world. We will vanish in thin air—think of it! Those left will not even be aware of the event until it is all over.

Since my childhood I have known about the scriptural teaching of the return of Christ. The circumstances that forcefully brought that truth to my young mind are indelibly stamped upon my consciousness. I was with Mother in the backyard of our home where she was sweeping leaves with a brush broom. Hearing a rumbling in the distance, she stopped sweeping, looked toward the East, the direction of the noise, where a thunderhead loomed. "Someday," she said in her saintly, quiet voice, "Christ is coming back, and He will come in a cloud, perhaps like that one," she concluded, as she pointed toward the thunderhead.

The rumbling, the cloud, and the thought of Christ appearing perturbed me, and all the while the noise in the cloud's direction became louder. Soon, however, my mind was set at ease, for I heard the faint, distant blowing of the whistle of a freight train, and I knew that the train accounted for the rumbling sound. Of course, soon afterward I learned that the Lord did not give the doctrine of the Rapture to frighten us, but for comfort and encouragement.

Others Have Been Raptured

The concept of being translated is hardly conceivable to you and me, for the only way we have seen people depart from this life has been through death. However, a few people in Biblical history did not die. They include Enoch, Elijah, and of course our Lord after His resurrection.

Jesus Spoke of His Return

The thoughts of our Lord dwelt often upon His second advent. Such statements as, "When the Son of Man shall come in his glory"; "The Son of Man shall come"; or "I will come again," intersperse His recorded sayings. The night before His ignominious death at Calvary, the Lord spoke tenderly to His disciples about His return. He endeavored to prepare them for His leaving by telling them why He was going and that He would come back. His compassionate words were spoken to His tired disciples on that dark night of the betrayal, and we look deep into His concerned heart as He endeavored to bolster the courage of His wavering disciples. He said: "Let not your heart be troubled. You are trusting God, now trust in me. There are

many homes up there where my Father lives, and I am going
to prepare them for your coming. When everything is ready,
then I will come and get you, so that you can always be with
me where I am. If this weren't so, I would tell you plainly"
(John 14:1–3 TLB).

Though His disciples did not comprehend the discussion that
night, how it must have buoyed their faith the following months
and years when they remembered His emphatic statement that
He would come again and take them away. Surely they anticipated His return every day. Christ will keep His word and
will come again for His disciples. They will arise at the resurrection at the Rapture; ". . . and the dead in Christ shall rise first,"
Paul wrote. Therefore, when Christ comes back, all of those
saints who have died since the cross will rise, and if you and
I are living for Him then, we will be translated, and together
we will all be taken by Christ to heaven. (See 1 Thessalonians
4:16, 17.)

The Lord's Supper Anticipates Christ's Return

Did you ever consider that when you participate in that very
sacred ordinance, the communion, you are giving testimony to
your faith in the return of Christ? Let us take a look at that first
supper. The twelve disciples met with the Lord in the upper
room for the evening meal. While the dining progressed Judas
pondered the betrayal and Christ knew his thoughts. The other
disciples were oblivious of the fact that their treasurer contem-
plated such a dastardly act.

The drama and suspense that transpired that evening could
never be fully reenacted on the stage nor even in the imagination. Jesus' heart was heavy. Added to the gigantic burden of

His imminent death was the heartbreak that one of His disciples would betray Him to His enemies, and that the others, one by one, would forsake Him and flee. Nonetheless, against this backdrop Jesus confidently instituted the Lord's Supper.

This holy event became an ordinance of the Church, and every time you and I take communion we are saying by our actions that Christ is coming back. The Bible declares it:

> . . . the Lord Jesus, in the night in which He was betrayed, took bread, and when He had given thanks He broke it and said, "(Take, eat) This is my body, broken on your behalf; this do in remembrance of Me." Similarly also (He took) the cup after they had supped, saying, "This cup is the new covenant in My blood. This do, as often as you drink it, in remembrance of Me. For as often as you eat this bread and drink the cup, you shall proclaim the Lord's death till He comes." (1 Corinthians 11:23-26 BERKELEY)

A sacred event took place in the Holy Land which you probably read about in the newspapers. Twelve hundred delegates to the Jerusalem Conference on Biblical Prophecy gathered on the Mount of Olives on June 18, 1971, to participate in a communion service, to remember the Lord's death "till He comes." The vast congregation partook of bread baked by Christian Arabs in Bethlehem and wine made from grapes grown on Mount Carmel, which they sipped from communion cups made from olive wood. The service took place on the very mountain from which Christ ascended to heaven and the same one to which He will return (Zechariah 14:4). Looking westward, the delegates had a breathtaking view of the holy city, dominated by the old temple area, which may be the exact site from which Christ will rule the world for a thousand years. The unity and brotherliness that pervaded that vast service as men and women from thirty-two different countries took the communion was a foretaste of the joy and oneness that will be in evidence as believers from around the world are caught away in the Rapture!

The New Testament Writers

Penning their thoughts under the inspiration of the Holy Spirit, the writers of the New Testament often referred to Christ's coming. Three hundred and nineteen verses are devoted to the subject. You will find that on the average one verse out of every twenty-five is given to the theme, making it a major doctrine of the New Testament. First and Second Thessalonians are generally conceded to have been the first two Pauline books written, and both of them clearly set forth the doctrine of the return of Christ. In fact, 1 Thessalonians 4:16, 17 could well be called the polestar reference concerning the translation of the Church. All of the Epistles anticipate the return of Christ, and the Book of Revelation is given almost entirely to His return and to the events following. Any serious student of the Bible must concede that the return of Jesus Christ is an emphatic theme of the New Testament.

Church Leaders Expected Jesus

Many of the Church leaders since Paul referred to the return of Christ. It should be stated, however, that some, but not all, of them were either amillennial or postmillennial, not premillennial as are almost all evangelicals today. In the first century

Ignatius of Antioch stated, "Christ was received up to the Father and sits on his right hand, waiting til his enemies are put under his feet." Irenaeus, who lived in the second century, said of Christ, "Appearing from heaven in the Glory of the Father, to comprehend all things under one head."

Through the centuries men have spoken of Christ's return. Though during the Dark Ages sight of "that blessed hope" was almost completely lost, later the doctrine was proclaimed again. It was said of Wycliffe, "[He] regarded the Redeemer's appearing as the object of the hope and constant expectation of the church of God."

John Calvin commented, "The Scripture uniformly commands us to look forward with eager expectation to the coming of Christ." John Knox testified, "We know that He shall return, and that with expedition." Martin Luther said, "I ardently hope that amidst these interval dissensions on earth, Jesus Christ will hasten the day of His coming." The great songs of Charles Wesley reverberate with the doctrine of the return of Christ. He wrote:

> O may we all be found
> Obedient to thy word,
> Attentive to the trumpets' sound,
> And looking for the Lord.

For centuries the church has recited the Apostles' Creed. Every time we recite it, we reaffirm our faith in Christ's return. It reads in part: "I believe in God the Father Almighty, and in Jesus Christ His only Son our Lord. He ascended into heaven, and sitteth on the right hand of God the Father Almighty. From thence He shall come to judge the quick and the dead."

We Expect Him to Return

When we speak of the imminent return of Jesus we mean that He could come at any time. As you understand, that time could be very soon. Many Christians feel that the event is quite probably upon us. On the other hand, we do not know when He will come. Time-wise, seventy-five years with God is almost as nothing while for us it is a life-span. However, signs foretold in the Scriptures such as those of the Tribulation, Armageddon, and the Second Coming of Christ to earth, cast distinct shadows on these days. Therefore, He could come at any moment.

Whereas a few years ago one seldom heard a sermon on the return of Christ, now evangelical preachers often refer to the Rapture, the Tribulation, Armageddon and the Millennium. There is a great deal of emphasis today upon things to come, and I believe the accelerated interest is the Holy Spirit's way of making us ever mindful of the Lord's imminent appearance. Billy Graham has said, "There is a foreboding in the air. Something phenomenal is about to happen; and that phenomenal happening will be the return of Christ." A national magazine recently stated, "For many, there exists a firm conviction that Jesus' Second Coming is literally at hand."

Something Is Going to Happen

Some people who do not necessarily accept the teachings of the Bible—in fact, who may not even be aware of the futuristic aspect of the Scriptures—are saying that something must happen, that a cataclysmic event of worldwide proportions is inevitable. You are probably aware that since the splitting of the atom, statesmen, scientists, politicians, and men from all other walks of life, have asked with increasing frequency, "Where are we headed? What can we do? When will the end occur?"

Churchill said, "Our problems are beyond us," while Jean-Paul Sartre commented, "There is no exit from the human dilemma." Evangelist Billy Graham in his book *World Aflame*, wrote, "Our world is filled with fear, hate, lust, greed, war and utter despair. Surely the Second Coming of Jesus Christ is the only hope of replacing these depressing features with trust, love, universal peace and prosperity. For it the world wittingly or inadvertently waits."

In this perplexing hour Christ could well return. At any moment the believers could be whisked from this sin-blighted world, for the Lord will come at a dark hour: "And that, knowing the time, that now it is high time to awake out of sleep: for now is our salvation nearer than when we believed. The night is far spent, the day is at hand: let us therefore cast off the works of darkness, and let us put on the armour of light" Romans 13:11, 12).

When Will Jesus Come?

Though we believe the coming of the Lord is near, we do not know when He will come. He could well come tonight or tomorrow. Nonetheless, we do not have any Biblical grounds to justify our setting a date, saying that Christ will return at a certain time. Foolish conjectures have been made in the past. For example, it has been projected that in God's own providence the measurements of the Great Pyramid in Egypt correspond with certain prophetic truths, and by studying these measurements one can ascertain the future. However, it seems unreasonable that God would use a tomb of a dead heathen king to show forth the return of His living Son!

Some people earnestly believed that Christ was going to return at a certain date during the last century. They either sold their property or gave it away, donned white robes, and went to mountaintops to await the appearance of the Lord. Further, the founder of the Jehovah's Witnesses sect, Judge Rutherford, said that Christ came in 1914, but that His coming was of a spiritual nature and none saw Him. God has not seen fit to adjust to men's foolish predictions. Jesus discussed this matter of our not knowing just when He would come back. He emphasized that neither the angels nor He Himself knew the date. Therefore He admonished you and me to "Watch therefore: for ye know not what hour your Lord doth come" (Matthew 24: 42).

Writing to the church at Thessalonica, the Apostle Paul emphasized that Christ would come unexpectedly. He said: "For yourselves know perfectly that the day of the Lord so cometh as a thief in the night" (1 Thessalonians 5:2). So we do not know just when Christ will come, but we do know that He will come unannounced and we believe that His coming is near.

Recently a woman in the state of Georgia dreamed that she died and went to heaven. Upon arrival she found decorations being mounted, a massive platform being built, and everyone was busily engaged in work. Finally, she got the attention of someone and asked why all the preparation and whether something unusual was about to happen. "Haven't you heard," her informant answered, "we believe that the Father is about to send the Son for His Bride, and we are preparing for the celebration."

What Will Happen When He Comes?

In His infinite wisdom the Holy Spirit did not reveal to us in the Scriptures *when* Christ would return. However, He was most explicit in telling us just *how* the Lord Jesus would return, spelling out the event step-by-step. That momentous occurrence is dramatically described by the writer Paul:

> One word of command, one shout from the archangel, one blast from the trumpet of God and the Lord Himself will come down from Heaven! Those who have died in Christ will be first to rise, and then we who are still living on the earth will be swept up with them into the clouds to meet the Lord in the air. And after that we shall be with him for ever. So by all means use this message to encourage one another. (1 Thessalonians 4:16–18 PHILLIPS)

Note the six emphatic points made in this reference: (1) The Lord Himself is coming back, (2) The dead in Christ shall rise first, (3) The Living shall be caught up, (4) We shall meet the Lord in the air, (5) We shall be with Christ forever, (6) We are to encourage each other with the message.

1. *The Lord Himself is coming back.* In the past some important Biblical events have been carried out by archangels. It seems that Michael's duty may have been to watch over the children of Israel (Daniel 12:1), while Gabriel has conveyed important messages to people in general. However, when the Rapture takes place, though an archangel is active, he is not the central figure. The Lord Himself is coming after us! The event is too important to entrust even to an archangel.

The same Jesus who was born of Mary, ministered in Palestine, died on Calvary, arose triumphantly, and ascended into the heavens—that same Jesus is coming again. The Lord Himself, the Christ who forgave your sins and mine, and to whom we have prayed since our conversion—He will descend from heaven.

2. *The dead in Christ shall rise first.* All of those who have died in the faith since Calvary will rise. Those dead outside of Christ will not rise until the Great White Throne Judgment after the Millennium (Revelation 20). My saintly mother, who was immobile for two years before dying, the result of a paralytic stroke, will arise with a sound body, with all signs of the paralyzed arm, foot, and tongue gone. She will be physically perfect. Dad, who was a vibrant witness for the Lord until his death, will be able to speak without stuttering, for that impediment will be gone. *The dead in Christ shall rise first.* Those who have died at sea, the thousands buried in the catacombs of Rome, and all the other dead in Christ will be raised to life.

3. *The living shall be caught up.* After the dead are raised, the living shall be changed "in a moment, in the twinkling of an eye" (1 Corinthians 15:52), without experiencing death. If you and I are living then and are dedicated to Christ we shall be changed instantly from mortals to immortals. Our bodies shall be made like Christ's glorious body; they will be immortal, perfect, painless, spiritual and eternal. The Scriptures describe our future bodies: "But we are citizens of Heaven; our outlook goes beyond this world to the hopeful expectation of the savior who will come from Heaven, the Lord Jesus Christ. He will change these wretched bodies of ours so that they resemble his own glorious body, by that power of his which makes him the master of everything that is" (Philippians 3:20,21 PHILLIPS).

4. *We shall meet the Lord in the air.* Paul said that we ". . . will be swept up with them [the resurrected] into the clouds to meet the Lord in the air" (1 Thessalonians 4:17 PHILLIPS). All of the true Christians—boys, girls, men and women—will be caught up. The unbelievers will be left on earth; the unregenerate dead will be left in the grave, but the dedicated followers of Christ will be raptured with them into the clouds.

This means that we will be reunited with our loved ones and friends who died in the faith. What a joyous occasion! Little wonder that the scriptural references confirming the Rapture often reflect exuberance and happiness, while those about the Second Coming of Christ to the earth speak of judgment and sternness which Christ will exercise in destroying His enemies.

After we have met our loved ones in the clouds, we shall meet the Lord in the air. The marvelous, compassionate Saviour who forgave our sins, Him shall we meet. The Lord Jesus whom we have accepted by faith and about whom we have witnessed, Him we shall see face-to-face. Imagine the excitement seeing Him for the first time. Surely we will:

> Bow down before Him,
> Love and adore Him
> His name is wonderful
> Jesus, my Lord.

> —AUDREY MIEIR

> © Copyright 1959 by Manna Music, Inc., N. Hollywood, Calif.

5. *We shall be with Christ forever.* Our seeing the Lord Jesus will not be just a temporary experience, but we will be in His holy presence forever. Think of it. We will dwell with Him, the essence of purity, holiness and intelligence. We will appear before Him as He sits on the Judgment Seat, and we shall accompany Him at the marriage supper. Then we will come with Him back to the earth and will reign with Him a thousand years here upon this earth. Then in the new heaven and new earth we shall forever be with the Lord.

What great dividends we will reap throughout eternity by accepting Him now and following His teaching during our short lifetime. Someday soon all of this life will be over. How eager we become at times to be with the Lord, where forever we will be in His presence. The psalmist must have had such a longing when he wrote: "As for me, I will behold thy face in righteousness: I shall be satisfied, when I awake, with thy likeness" (Psalms 17:15).

6. *We are to encourage each other with the message.* It is a blessed privilege for you and me to encourage each other in the faith. When the burdens are heavy and the tempest is raging, the believer should be told that Jesus says, "Behold I come quickly: hold that fast which thou hast, that no man take thy crown" (Revelation 3:11). When our way is involved and our vision is earthbound, we are admonished to keep our faith heavenward for ". . . unto them that look for him shall he appear the second time without sin unto salvation" (Hebrews 9:28). When critics say that Christ is not coming, we should not waver but remember: "For yet a little while, and he that shall come will come, and will not tarry" (Hebrews 10:37).

Unwavering faith in the return of Christ makes for sturdy, healthy Christians. I do not know one believer who faithfully anticipates Christ's return, but that he is a confident, productive disciple. The Book of Hebrews calls our hope in the future an anchor of the soul: "Which hope we have as an anchor of the soul, both sure and stedfast, and which entereth into that within the veil; Whither the forerunner is for us entered, even Jesus, made an high priest for ever after the order of Melchisedec" (Hebrews 6:19, 20).

How Should We Live Now?

Speaking to a group of church leaders in Wheaton, Illinois, in September of 1971, Dr. Kenneth Gangel declared, "The New Testament abounds with references of God's demands for holiness." This fact is certainly evident in many of the references concerning Christ's return. Careless living and indifference toward the things of God are not the marks of one who is looking for that blessed hope. Christ is coming after people who are right with Him; those who worship Him and prayerfully follow His teachings.

Note what the Scriptures say:

> When Christ, who is our life, shall appear, then shall ye also appear with him in glory. Mortify therefore your members which are upon the earth; fornication, uncleanness, inordinate affection, evil concupiscence, and covetousness. (Colossians 3:4,5)

> Beloved, now are we the sons of God, and it doth not yet appear what we shall be: but we know that, when he shall appear, we shall be like him; for we shall see him as he is. And every man that hath this hope in him purifieth himself, even as he is pure. (1 John 3:2, 3)

These references suggest that Christ is coming after people who are living careful, godly lives and who are pure of heart. In fact, a criterion for living with God eternally, whether we go to heaven by death or the Rapture, was stated by our Lord as one of the beatitudes. He said, "Blessed are the pure in heart: for they shall see God" (Matthew 5:8).

Nonetheless, it will be the righteousness of God in us that will make us eligible for the Rapture. I, for one, am certainly gratified that requirements will not be based on our personal goodness. If so, I would be left when Jesus comes. Prayerful, godly, righteous living, while trusting in the finished work of Calvary, will render us eligible to go. Therefore, we will go in the Rapture as the result of our confessing our sins to Christ, accepting Him into our hearts, and carefully following Him day-by-day.

Three Greek Words

Mention should be made of three words used in the New Testament in reference to the coming of Christ.

1. *Parousia.* Being used about twenty-five times in the New Testament, it is the one word employed most frequently to describe the return of our Lord. It carries the idea of personal presence, meaning that Christ will return in person. (See 1 Corinthians 15:23; I Thessalonians 2:9; James 5:7,8; I John 2:29.)

2. *Epiphaneia.* Carrying the concept of appearing, this word means appearing out of darkness. Such will be the case when Christ, the bright and morning Star, appears in this dark world. Some passages where it is used referring to the Rapture are: 1 Timothy 6:14; 2 Timothy 4:8.

3. *Apokalupsis.* This word means to reveal or unveil. Today Christ is hidden from view; He is with us by faith. When He returns He will be revealed in person. The word is used in these passages when referring to the Rapture: 1 Corinthians 1:7; Colossians 3:4; 1 Peter 1:7, 13.

Rapture Before the Tribulation?

When a person states that he believes that the Bible teaches the Rapture of the Church, it does not necessarily follow that he agrees with everyone else as to the time in the future that the Lord will return. There are four different views concerning the Rapture:

1. *Pre-Tribulation Rapture.* The Bible refers to the Tribula-

tion as being the most dreadful days that ever existed. Matthew, chapter 24, records Christ's graphic description of that seven-year period, and the Revelation states: "For the great day of his wrath is come; and who shall be able to stand" (Revelation 6:17). The pre-Tribulationist cannot comprehend the Church going through God's wrath. Instead, he anticipates the return of Christ who "delivered us from the wrath to come" (1 Thessalonians 1:10). Most evangelical Christians expect Christ to return before the Tribulation, hence they are pre-Tribulationists.

2. *Partial Rapture*. Quite a few dedicated, Bible-loving Christians hold this view. They are pre-Tribulationists, but believe that the Scriptures teach that only the zealous, the holiest of the holy, will be worthy of the Rapture.

3. *Mid-Tribulation Rapture*. Holding that Christ will return after the first three and one half years of the Tribulation, adherents to this view teach that the Church is promised Tribulation and is in need of it for purging; that the Rapture will then take place, removing the Church from the world so that the latter and more dreadful half of the Tribulation can run its course.

4. *Post-Tribulation Rapture*. This view holds that the Church will remain on the earth throughout the Tribulation, at the end of which the Church will be raptured to meet the Lord in the air, who will be on His way from heaven to earth. The Church will join Christ and return to the earth with Him.

What do I believe? As most evangelical Christians, I am persuaded that the Bible teaches the Rapture could take place at any moment, which would be before the Tribulation begins. Who will go? If our hearts are right with the Lord when He comes, we will go; if not, we will be passed by. We can go; we must go! We just cannot afford to miss the Rapture.

The Holy Spirit used the doctrine of the Rapture to lead me

to Christ. He pierced my heart with this truth one wintry Sunday afternoon while as a teen-ager I was sitting around the fireplace while still living at home with my parents. As was customary, Dad was talking of spiritual things, and on that particular day his mind dwelt upon the Rapture. He said, "You know, it is going to be bad to be good, but not good enough to go." Dad was perceptive, and he may have sensed my spiritual need. On the other hand, he may not have been aware of my need of Christ, for I went to church, sang in the choir, and did not have many of the open habits common to the unconverted. I was a good boy, but I had never had a personal encounter with Christ. I was good, but not good enough; I had not been born again.

Upon retirement that night, sleep fled, and my youthful heart, convicted of its sins, beat out the stinging truth, "It is going to be bad to be good, but not good enough to go." The following weekend during a communion service I gave my heart to Christ.

> I do not know how soon 'twill be
> That my dear Lord will come for me;
> But this I know, 'twill all be well
> For I shall ever with Him dwell.
>
> Then hark, my soul! Awake! Rejoice!
> He'll come again; I'll hear His voice;
> And rise with millions, bright and fair,
> To meet my Saviour in the air.
>
> —OSWALD J. SMITH

3
This Is Your Life

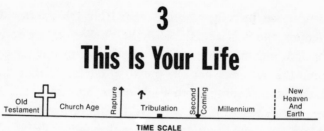

TIME SCALE
The arrow (↑) indicates the location of this study.

If you and I go in the Rapture with Christ, we will live in heaven for seven years while the Tribulation takes place here on earth (Daniel 9:27). While up there we will appear before the Judgment Seat of Christ, attend the marriage supper of the Lamb, and then come back to the earth with the Messiah when He returns to rule the world for a thousand years.

Our finite minds cannot comprehend the glories that await us in heaven. Surely that place will be much more than we can even imagine it to be. For one thing, we will have time to associate more with each other. Years ago there was a quaint gospel song that spoke beautifully of our lives in heaven. The chorus went as follows:

> Here you meet me as a stranger on the highways,
> Never stopping, never asking my name,
> But in heaven we will all get well acquainted,
> You will love me and I'll love you the same;
> I will "hail you" and you'll answer like a brother,
> Many blessings in the garden we'll share,
> In that city when we all move close together
> You will be my closest neighbor up there!

> —ALBERT E. BRUMLEY

Also, we will be in the presence of the Holy Trinity, including the Father, the Son, and the Holy Spirit. We will freely bow down and worship. Our limited minds can not at all comprehend the harmony nor the purity of our association there with the Holy Trinity, with each other, and with the holy angels. Nonetheless, if we will live for the Lord during our earthly life, we will some day dwell in that indescribable place that He has prepared for us.

What Is Heaven Like?

I do not believe that life in heaven is altogether as we sometimes hear it described, for I doubt that we will only sit and strum on a harp while shading our eyes from glistening streets of gold. We may have harps and streets of gold, but that is not all there is to heaven. In fact, that may only be a caricature of our waiting home. Rather, heaven is a place of action. We will be busy praising, serving, visiting and worshiping.

Someone said that the door to heaven may have a sign reading, "No admission except on business." Pointing up our activity there, the Scriptures state: ". . . his servants shall serve him" (Revelation 22:3).

Heaven is also a place of unimagined beauty. John, the writer of Revelation, described it as a bride adorned for her husband (Revelation 21:2). Think of the sheer beauty of a meticulously dressed bride meeting the groom. Womanhood is never lovelier than at that time. The Holy Spirit uses that illustration to put us in the proper frame of mind to ponder the beauty of heaven.

A little girl was quiet for an unusually long period of time while strolling on a clear night with her father. Finally he asked what was on her mind. "I was just thinking," the child answered, "if heaven with its stars is so beautiful wrong side out, how wonderful it must be on the other side."

The Bible Tells Us of Heaven

The holy Scriptures point out that heaven will be our dwelling place immediately after the Rapture (John 14:1–4) and that the Antichrist will curse us during the Tribulation, ". . . them that dwell in the heaven" (Revelation 13:6). Numerous names are applied to our future home, such as: "my Father's house" (John 14:2); "a city which hath foundations" (Hebrews 11:10); "mount Sion" (Hebrews 12:22); and "that great city" (Revelation 21:10).

Apparently we, the redeemed since the cross, will occupy the most intimate place with Jesus Christ (Revelation 3:21). When the Old Testament saints are resurrected, apparently at the end of the Tribulation when Christ returns to the earth (Daniel 12:1,2; Hebrews 11:40), they will enjoy the city of God during the Millennium and afterward. Apparently, they will be next to us in importance at that time. Thirdly, innumerable angels will be present in heaven (Hebrews 12:22) for the precise purpose of serving us (Hebrews 1:14).

A Look At Your Life

Did you know that when you get to heaven after the Rapture you will be judged by Christ Himself? So will we all, for our acts during our Christian life will be evaluated. Just as a popular television show reviews the life of an individual, recalling persons and events which the individual may have nearly forgotten, so will our Christian lives be reviewed by Christ. The difference in the heavenly "This Is Your Life" will be that every unpleasant aspect will be aired, as well as the praiseworthy ones, "whether it be good or bad." Our conduct back on earth will be reviewed: "For we must all appear before the judgment seat of Christ; that every one may receive the things done in his body, according to that he hath done, whether it be good or bad" (2 Corinthians 5:10).

While walking along a New York City street recently, I was appalled at the audaciousness of a teen-age gang. The youths were throwing long passes with a football up and down the busy thoroughfare, while cars swerved or screeched to a halt to avoid hitting them. Language was foul and tenseness pervaded the air.

In these surroundings, I suddenly came upon a grand old church, Calvary Baptist, which I knew had been a lighthouse to many wandering souls. Having heard the pastor, Stephen Olford, preach, I knew his belief in Christ as both Saviour and Judge. He wrote recently in *Prophecy and the Seventies* about the Judgment Seat of Christ: "The Judgment Seat of Christ is an intensely solemn and searching aspect of prophetic truth. On account of this, it is not popular either in public preaching or in private discussion."

You see, this will not be a judgment of your sins, but of your service. If Christ the righteous Judge finds you worthy, He will present rewards gratuitously for faithful works. Paul referred to this judgment in his letter to the Romans: "But why dost thou judge thy brother? or why dost thou set at nought thy brother? for we shall all stand before the judgment seat of Christ" (Romans 14:10).

Have You Heard About the Bema?

In New Testament times the *bema,* or *reward seat,* rested on a raised platform in the arena where sports events were held.

The president or umpire sat on the bema where he watched the games, and from which he presented rewards to the winning athletes. The bema was never used as a judicial bench, but only as a reward seat.

Likewise, the Judgment Seat, or bema, of Christ will not be for the purpose of judging our sins, but to reward us for our service. The songs you sang for His glory, the Sunday-school class you taught, the sick you visited—if you did these things for Christ's praise and not for ulterior motives, they will bring rewards. What a soul-searching time it will be at the bema!

The Judgment Seat of Christ will not convene to ascertain whether we will go to heaven, for we will already be there. Nor will it be to determine whether we will be removed and cast into hell. No, this will be a judgment of our Christian living, not for wrongs committed. We have already been forgiven for our sins, and we do not have to face judgment for them.

Our Three Judgments

While those who die outside of Christ will not be judged until after the Millennium, when they will be resurrected and judged at the great white throne (Revelation 20:11–15), we will not be judged at that judgment. Nonetheless, we do face judgments.

1. *Judged as sinners, a past judgment.* Before we accepted Christ we were already judged as sinners. Jesus Himself said, ". . . he that believeth not is condemned already . . ." (John 3:18). Being apart from God, we were under His wrath; we were judged. But then we repented of our sins, and accepted Christ's atoning work for us, and we became His followers. Paul wrote: "There is therefore now no condemnation [judgment] to them which are in Christ Jesus . . ." (Romans 8:1), while the psalmist said: "As far as the east is from the west, so far hath he removed

our transgressions from us" (Psalms 103:12). Our sins are for-gotten. We shall not be judged for them.

2. *Judged as sons, a present judgment.* The Heavenly Father through the Holy Spirit constantly judges us, reminding us that "This is the way, walk ye in it." The Bible declares: ". . . My son, despise not thou the chastening of the Lord, nor faint when thou art rebuked of him: For whom the Lord loveth he chas-teneth, and scourgeth every son whom he receiveth" (Hebrews 12:5,6).

3. *Judged as servants, a future judgment.* This judgment is yet to come, and it will take place at the Judgment Seat of Christ.

The Bema Bares Our Lives

The omniscient Christ will be the Judge at the bema, for only Deity would be at all capable of carrying out the judging of the millions of people who will stand before the Judgment Seat. The Bible teaches that He will: ". . . bring to light the hidden things of darkness, and will make manifest the counsels of the hearts: and then shall every man have praise of God" (1 Corinthians 4:5).

The Sovereign Saviour will bring to surface our hidden mo-tives, whether good or bad, and He will show the inner thoughts of our hearts. This will be a completely impartial and just decision. Sometimes we are misunderstood and misjudged by people, but Christ will not misjudge.

Have you wondered just how this judgment will take place? The Scriptures are quite explicit in telling us. The Record reads:

For none is able to lay another foundation than the one already laid, which is Jesus Christ. In case one builds on

> this foundation gold, silver, precious stones, wood, hay, stubble, each one's work will come to evidence, for the Day will bring it to light; by fire it shall be revealed. Of whatever quality each one's work may be, the fire will test it. In case one's construction survives, he will receive pay. In case one's work is burned down, he will be the loser; though personally he will be saved, yet only as passing through fire. (1 Corinthians 3:11–15 BERKELEY)

It is generally conceded that gold, silver and precious stones denote service done for God's glory. On the other hand, wood, hay and stubble, though also representing work done, probably will be service rendered without giving the Lord praise due Him. Things done in His vineyard, yet performed for our own aggrandizement, will be in the wood, hay and stubble category, and will be burned up. The fire on that day must mean the searching judgment of God, "For our God is a consuming fire" (Hebrews 12:29).

Note that verse 15 of Corinthians reads, "In case one's work is burned down, he will be the loser; though personally he will be saved, yet only as passing through fire." Really, this verse cuts close, inferring that it may be possible to stay busy in God's work, and yet have most of our service "burned up" at the Judgment Seat. May God help us not to witness, sing, pray, or preach just to pull attention to ourselves or to further our own ends, but rather may we work to bring praise to Christ, for He only is worthy of all praise and glory.

Our Works Burned

We hear a good deal about our rewards in heaven, but very little about our losses. I do not know what is meant by the statement, "In case one's work is burned down, he will be the loser." I do not know just how we will suffer shame and embarrassment in heaven, but this reference infers that we will. Things that we do here to glorify the flesh, regardless of what the deed may be, will be disapproved on that day.

In his *God's Plan of the Ages,* Louis T. Talbot wrote: "All the unknown and unsung words and deeds of mercy; all the silent praises and prayers; all the selfish motives and idle words and bitter thoughts—these will go on parade before the all-seeing eye of the Son of God. What a solemn thought this is!"

The Lord will require of us according to our ability. It has been said, "God never looks at the amount on the face of the check, but He looks at the balance on the stub." The Bible is clear on the point that if we are to be rewarded at the Judgment Seat of Christ, we must render dedicated, Christ-honoring service during this life.

The Five Crowns

God's Word refers to our rewards at the bema as crowns. Apparently this means rewards such as the victory wreaths and crowns given in games during New Testament times (1 Corinthians 9:25; 2 Timothy 2:5), or the golden crown proposed for Demosthenes, the Athenian, as a reward for his distinguished public service. The crowns awarded at the bema will not be of the kingly sort, for the king's crown is reserved only for Christ the King of kings. Our rewards will be victor's crowns, such as those the elders cast at the feet of Christ in worship and adoration (Revelation 4:10). The rewards we are to receive are catagorized in five general areas.

1. *The incorruptible crown.* Mentioned in 1 Corinthians 9:25, this reward is bestowed for getting mastery over the "old man,"

and it awaits each of us who lives for the Lord with singleness of purpose. We are to live daily with the goal in mind, being temperate in all things.

2. *The crown of rejoicing.* This is a special reward for soul-winners. First Thessalonians 2:19,20 affirms that souls won for our Master will make us worthy of this crown. What an award must await the Apostle Paul, not only for the Thessalonians whom he had won to the Lord, but for all the host of others he had led to Calvary. Daniel, of the Old Testament, wrote: "And they that be wise shall shine as the brightness of the firmament: and they that turn many to righteousness as the stars for ever and ever" (Daniel 12:3).

The Spirit may have had the crown of rejoicing in mind when He moved Apostle John to write: "Behold, I come quickly: hold that fast which thou hast, that no man take thy crown" (Revelation 3:11).

Louis T. Talbot told of a man who stood on a street corner years ago handing out Christian literature. A man going home from work took one of the Christian tracts, read it, was convicted of his sins, and gave his heart to Christ. The new convert went back to the street corner to thank his benefactor for giving him the tract, but the man was not there. After several trips the new convert concluded that the Christian worker was either ill or had moved, so he secured tracts and began to regularly hand them out on the same street corner.

Later in a prayer meeting he related the account of his conversion and subsequent ministry with the tracts and his unknown benefactor was in the congregation. His benefactor stood and said, "My friend, I got discouraged and gave up the tract ministry as useless—and now you have taken my crown." May the Lord help us to serve patiently and faithfully in the area that He has placed us.

3. *The crown of life.* James 1:12 states that if we will endure the trials of this life, we will receive a crown of life, "which the Lord hath promised to them that love him." When Satan storms the walls of our souls, threatening to break through, we must stand firm, trusting in the strength of Christ, remembering that, "Blessed is the man that endureth temptation: for when he is tried, he shall receive the crown of life."

4. *The crown of righteousness.* What a reassuring reference is found in Paul's second letter to Timothy. It states that a reward has already been laid aside for us if we eagerly look for Christ to return. It reads: ". . . there is laid up for me a crown of righteousness, which the Lord, the righteous judge, shall give me at that day: and not to me only, but unto all them also that love his appearing" (2 Timothy 4:8).

The saintly Paul, just before his decapitation, anticipated the crown of righteousness. Nonetheless, he will not receive it until "that day"; that is, until he stands before the Judgment Seat of Christ.

5. *The crown of glory.* This seems to be a special reward for the faithful pastor who willingly feeds his flock week after week. The Apostle Peter discussed the reward as follows: "I appeal to the elders among you: shepherd God's flock that is with you, not because you have to, but because with God you want to; not out of greed for gain, but eagerly; not lording it over your charges, but becoming examples to your flock. And with the appearing of the Chief Shepherd you will be awarded the never-fading crown of glory" (1 Peter 5:2–4 BERKELEY).

This never-fading crown is promised as a reward for unselfish, exemplary pastoral ministry. Many faithful men of God will receive this crown. Dedicated pastors who spend hours in prayer about sermons, about burdens of their members, and about spiritual needs of their congregation will be candidates for this reward. It is understandable that God has a special honor for the pastors who marry the young, bury the dead, comfort the brokenhearted, and lead sinners to the Lord Jesus. These unsung heroes who have cared for God's flock that has been entrusted to them will be honored by Christ at the Judgment Seat.

Before leaving our discussion of the Judgment Seat of Christ we should take a look at the Scripture's warning to us not to judge our brother, but to leave judgment to Christ to be carried out at the bema.

We Must Not Judge Our Brother

The Lord knows how human it is for us to criticize our fellow Christians. It is so easy for me to clearly see the mote in your eye, while completely ignoring the beam in my own! Understandably, Christ called such biased attitudes sheer hypocrisy. The Living Bible gives the Lord's words as follows: "Don't criticize, and then you won't be criticized. For others will treat you as you treat them. And why worry about a speck in the eye of a brother when you have a board in your own? Should you say, 'Friend, let me help you get that speck out of your eye,' when you can't even see because of the board in your own? Hypocrite! First get rid of the board. Then you can see to help your brother" (Matthew 7:1–5 TLB).

"For the Father . . . hath committed all judgment unto the Son" (John 5:22), and Paul asked, "But why dost thou judge thy brother? or why dost thou set at nought thy brother? for we shall all stand before the judgment seat of Christ" (Romans 14:10). Later Paul reminds us: ". . . he that judgeth me is the Lord. Therefore judge nothing before the time, until the Lord come, who both will bring to light the hidden things of darkness, and will make manifest the counsels of the hearts: and then shall every man have praise of God" (1 Corinthians 4:4, 5).

Romans 14:1–13 discusses the problem of Christians judging one another. The followers being addressed were concerned about eating certain things and observing certain days, and they were referred to as weak and strong. Paul admonished them to receive the weak brother (v. 1), because "God hath received him" (v.3), and he reminded them that they were not their brother's Lord (v.4.). Then Paul admonished them not to judge a brother, "for we must all stand before the judgment seat of Christ" (v.10).

The story is told of a woman who looked from her kitchen window one morning at her neighbor's white clothes hanging on the line next door. She remarked, "Just look at the dingy spots on her sheets. Why doesn't she bleach them?" "The spots," a friend countered, "are not on your neighbor's sheets; they are on your windowpanes!"

Likewise, we are prone to be the most critical when we have the most unconfessed faults. Instead of sitting in judgment against each other, may we encourage and strengthen the brother who appears to be weak; then at the Judgment Seat Christ will not have to judge us for judging a fellow believer.

The Wedding Banquet

After we are judged and rewarded by our Lord, and before returning to the earth with Christ, we will attend the marriage supper of the Lamb. The Bible calls the Church the bride of Christ, and the marriage supper will be a festive event celebrating the union of the Bridegroom with His bride. " 'Let us be glad and rejoice and honor him; for the time has come for the wedding banquet of the Lamb, and his bride has prepared herself. She is permitted to wear the cleanest and whitest and finest of linens.' (Fine linens represents the good deeds done by the people of God)" (Revelation 19:7,8 TLB).

That will be the greatest banquet ever held! It happens that I am writing these immediate lines while attending a convention in Chicago. Tonight hundreds of us were at a banquet convening in the massive ballroom of this large hotel. It was one of those above average banquets. The youth singing group was excellent, the food was good (which is not usual at banquets!) and the address by Dr. Richard Halverson of true humanity was provocative and inspiring. But one of these days I will attend another banquet where Christ Himself will be the host and where not just hundreds, but millions will be in attendance. That will be the marriage supper of the Lamb!

Time of the Supper.

The joyous event will take place between the Rapture and the Second Coming of Christ to the earth. It is apparent that the supper follows the *bema*, for the bride " '. . . is permitted to wear the cleanest and whitest and finest of linens.' (Fine linen represents the good deeds done by the people of God.)" This infers that the Church has been accepted and rewarded at the Judgment Seat.

Place of the Supper.

This banquet will take place in heaven. No other location could qualify for such a heavenly occasion. The Judgment Seat is in heaven, and after the marriage supper Christ returns to earth, so the event has to transpire in glory.

And in that holy company,
May you and I find place,
Through worth of Him who died for us,
And through His glorious grace;
With cherubim and seraphim,
And hosts of ransomed men,
To sing our praises to the Lamb,
And add our glad Amen.

4
Meanwhile Back on Earth

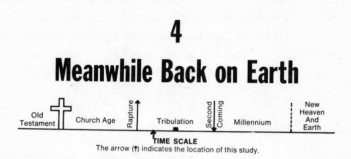

Old Testament | Church Age | Rapture | Tribulation | Second Coming | Millennium | New Heaven And Earth

TIME SCALE
The arrow (↑) indicates the location of this study.

When you consider that most of the earth's population does not even profess to be Christian, you soon realize that the vast majority of people will be left here when Christ takes His Church out of the world. As was pointed out earlier, a prerequisite for going in the Rapture is to be a believer, for that holy company will be comprised only of those who have been redeemed by Christ. (See Hebrews 9:28; Titus 2:12,13.)

Those Who Are Left

If Christ should come today and take to heaven all of those who know Him, the processes of world society would probably function practically normally tomorrow, for probably 80 or 90 percent or more of those who are here today would still be here to carry on. Though an innumerable host would go with Christ, multiplied millions would still be left here. Just as in Noah's day almost nobody believed that the flood was coming, likewise today people do not believe that Christ will come again.

Many may give mental assent to the Biblical truth, yet they have not turned to the Lord in preparation for His coming.

51

Jesus said: "And as it was in the days of Noe, so shall it be also in the days of the Son of man. Likewise also as it was in the days of Lot; they did eat, they drank, they bought, they sold, they planted, they builded; But the same day that Lot went out of Sodom it rained fire and brimstone from heaven, and destroyed them all. Even thus shall it be in the day when the Son of man is revealed" (Luke 17:26, 28–30).

Where Did They All Go?

Though most businesses, plants and schools will probably function as usual the day after the Rapture, it will still be a time of worldwide consternation. We can easily imagine all kinds of reports being given concerning the multiplied thousands of missing persons.

"Our weekly Optimist Club luncheon was in session and Joe was giving a report on our assistance to the Boys' Club when between words he was gone—just like that!—vanished while we were looking at him!"

"I had come home from the office for lunch, and my husband had picked up the baby at the nursery and we ate together. Before returning to work I stepped into the bedroom for a moment, and when I came out Jim and the baby were gone. Jim never just walked out like that. I don't understand it. They couldn't evaporate in thin air—or could they?"

"All of our news this evening will be given to the so-called Great Disappearance that took place at noon today. Also, all of our regular programming for the evening has been cancelled in order that we may keep you informed as news comes in about this most unusual worldwide event."

Analysts and philosophers will give their explanation of the mass disappearance, while people throughout the world will search for their missing friends and loved ones. However, like Enoch, they will not be found, for Christ will have taken them to heaven so that they might escape the horrendous times that will follow here upon earth.

Jesus Called It The Tribulation.

After the Church is taken out of the world, evil will begin to run rampant upon the earth. Besides, God will pour judgments upon the world. Christ referred to those days as Tribulation, and in the Olivet Discourse (Matthew 24), He talked at length about that terrible time. In fact, the seven-year period will contain the most trying days that ever existed, and there will never be times like them again.

We thought that Hitler's Auschwitz or Japan's concentration camps during World War II were unspeakably merciless, but Jesus said the Tribulation will be worse: "It will be a time of great distress; there has never been such a time from the beginning of the world until now, and will never be again. If that time of troubles were not cut short, no living thing could survive; but for the sake of God's chosen it will be cut short" (Matthew 24:21,22 NEB).

During that fearful period millions of people will die (Revelation 6:8) and others will desire to die, but death will flee (Revelation 9:6). The Tribulation is so important that most of Revelation (chapters 6–19) is given to a thorough discussion of it; further, part of the Book of Daniel describes it, while numerous references are made to it in as many places in the Bible. (See Isaiah 11:10, 11; Jeremiah 30:7; Ezekiel 38:16; Malachi 4:5.)

Not only does the last book of the Bible discuss the apostate religious system, the Antichrist, and the false prophet, but it also graphically details the judgments of God upon a Christ-rejecting world. It describes those judgments as seals (Revelation 6), trumpets (Revelation 8:2, 11:15), and bowls or vials (Revelation 16:1–21). God's other judgments are upon the apostate church (Revelation 17) and upon the Beast (Revelation 18).

The first of these judgments, the seals, could start happening very soon; that is, immediately after the Rapture. In his book *When Dust Shall Sing,* George Britt wrote, "Many discerning Bible students today can see the storm clouds of the Tribulation already gathering and casting their shadows upon this troubled, perplexed world."

Daniel of the Lions' Den

Since your early childhood you have heard of Daniel in the den of lions. God's locking their jaws and bringing Daniel out unscathed makes for a stirring and graphic story from God's Word. The account is found in chapter 6 of his book, and you will recall that the whole episode came about because Daniel was a man of prayer. He refused to pass up his prayer time even though he knew that the act of praying would lead him from the king's palace to the lion's den; he valued prayer higher than life itself.

Though most of us know about the lion's den of chapter 6, fewer of us know about the Seventy Weeks of chapter 9. However, that history-making experience came about also because Daniel was a man of prayer. Note that in the first few verses of the chapter the prophet was reading in the Book of Jeremiah, part of his Bible of that day. Then he sought God in prayer and fasting. It reads: ". . . I, Daniel, learned from the book of Jeremiah the prophet, that Jerusalem must lie desolate for seventy years. So I earnestly pleaded with the Lord God [to end our captivity and send us back to our own land]. As I prayed, I fasted, and wore rough sackcloth, and sprinkled myself with ashes, and confessed my sins and those of my people" (Daniel 9:2–4 TLB).

This grand old prophet—Berkeley says he was at least eighty-four years old—had learned the combination that unlocks the door to spiritual opportunities; that is, he had learned to study the Bible and pray. Though he lived more than two thousand years ago he had come upon this ever current formula that led him to spiritual heights with God. That same time-tested formula will still work today for you and me.

Read Daniel's prayer in Chapter 9; hear him as he confesses his sins and those of his people; feel his heartthrob as he implores God in verse 19: "O Lord, hear! O Lord, forgive! O God, take notice and take action; for Thine own sake, O God, do not delay; for Thy city and Thy people are called by Thy name" (BERKELEY).

If your prayer life is weak, give yourself to the quiet and consistent reading of the Bible. It was after reading God's Word that Daniel was moved to pray the great prayer of chapter 9. Also, it was after this time of Bible reading and prayer that he was morally and spiritually prepared to receive the revelation of the incredible prophecy known as the Seventy Weeks.

What Gabriel Told Daniel

In just four verses of chapter 9 the angel gave Daniel a panoramic view of things to come from Daniel's day until the cross, plus seven years that will take place in the future. The message brought by Gabriel to Daniel is as follows:

Seventy weeks are determined upon thy people and upon thy holy city, to finish the transgression, and to make an end of sins, and to make reconciliation for iniquity, and to bring in everlasting righteousness, and to seal up the vision and prophecy, and to anoint the most Holy. Know therefore and understand, that from the going forth of the commandment to restore and to build Jerusalem unto the Messiah the Prince shall be seven weeks, and threescore and two weeks: the street shall be built again, and the wall, even in troublous times. And after threescore and two weeks shall Messiah be cut off, but not for himself: and the people of the prince that shall come shall destroy the city and the sanctuary; and the end thereof shall be with a flood, and unto the end of the war desolations are determined. And he shall confirm the covenant with many for one week: and in the midst of the week he shall cause the sacrifice and the oblation to cease, and for the overspreading of abominations he shall make it desolate, even until the consummation, and that determined shall be poured upon the desolate. (Daniel 9:24–27)

Of course, you noticed the use of the term *weeks* in this passage. What does it mean? The Hebrew word used here for *week* is *heptad,* meaning a unit of measure, just as we use the term *dozen,* meaning twelve. In the case of Daniel's Seventy Weeks, a week is equal to seven years, with each day standing for a year.

The concept of a week meaning seven years was not new to the people of Israel. You will remember that when Jacob had worked seven years for Rachel and was given Leah instead, Laban told Jacob: "Fulfil her week, and we will give thee this also for the service which thou shalt serve with me yet seven other years. And Jacob did so, and fulfilled her week: and he gave him Rachel his daughter to wife also" (Genesis 29:27, 28). This account along with other Old Testament passages gives testimony to the fact that the Jews recognized they could have a week of days or a week of years.

The Three Divisions

Keep in mind that Gabriel foretold a span of time 490 years in length, divided as follows: (1) 7 weeks, or 49 years; (2) 62 weeks, or 434 years; and (3) 1 week, or 7 years.

(1) *The forty-nine years.* Daniel's Seventy Weeks are primarily directed, not to you and me, but to the Jews. The prophecy speaks of *thy people, thy holy city, the most Holy, the Messiah, covenant, sacrifice,* and *oblation.* These are Jewish terms directed to the Jewish people. Nonetheless, the prophecy, especially the seventieth week, ultimately has to do with all mankind. The "forty-nine years" reference of verse 25 is significant, for did you know that from the time permission was given Nehemiah to rebuild the wall and city of Jerusalem until it was finished was forty-nine years (about 445–396 B.C.)?

(2) *The 434 years.* These years date from the completion of the rebuilding of Jerusalem until Christ died at Calvary. Again, there were exactly 434 years of 360 days each between these events, just as Gabriel predicted. Chronologists such as Sir Robert Anderson testify to the dating of the Seventy Weeks. How amazingly accurate is God's Word!

(3) *The seven years.* This period will be discussed later, but suffice it here to remind you that this is the only part of Daniel's prophecy which has not been fulfilled. Since the sixty-nine "weeks" were fulfilled to the letter, we have little difficulty

believing that God will see to it that this last week will also take
place. This will be "the time of Jacob's trouble" (Jeremiah
30:7), "the Tribulation" (Matthew 24:29), and that horrid
period discussed in most of the Revelation (chapters 6–19).

The Great Parenthesis

You can readily see that Daniel's sixty-ninth week ended
when our Lord died at Calvary—when He was "cut off." At
that time the Jewish clock stopped; it has not sounded a tick
since Jesus said, "It is finished" (John 19:30), and dropped His
holy head and died. We are now living in an interpolation, a
time which Old Testament prophets did not mention or see
(Ephesians 3). We call this parenthesis time the Church age, a
time when, though the individual Jew may come to Christ if he
desires, this age of grace turned from the Jewish nation to the
Gentiles.

This gap between Daniel's sixty-ninth and seventieth weeks
is an indefinite period of time and will end when the Rapture
takes place. Then Daniel's seventieth week will start, and will
continue for a "week" or seven years. After the Rapture it will
be as though God reaches down and starts the pendulum of the
ancient Jewish clock, which will measure that last week.

The Week That Will Be

Daniel's Seventieth Week (Daniel 9:24–27), is the same
period discussed in Christ's Olivet Discourse (Matthew 24) and
John's seals, trumpets, and vials (Revelations, chapters 6–19).
With remarkably few words, Daniel gives us a panoramic view
of that time which we call the Tribulation. First, you will note
that he tells us why it will take place (verse 24); that is, "to

finish the transgression." Though the Jewish nation rejected Christ at Calvary, they will complete their transgression during the Tribulation. When Christ returns to the earth at the close of the Tribulation, He will "make an end of sins," for the Jews will accept His atoning work done at Calvary. Then He will "bring in everlasting righteousness," meaning His thousand-year millennial reign. At that time Daniel's prophecy will be finished, and the "most Holy" will be anointed. This anointing refers either to an anointing of Christ, or to the anointing of the holies in the Temple in the Millennium; the majority of evangelical opinion leans toward the latter interpretation.

Verse 26 refers to the fall of Jerusalem in A.D. 70. The "prince" of that verse refers to a world ruler during the Tribulation whom the Bible calls the Antichrist. But you should note that the phrase reads, "the people of the prince." It is believed that the Antichrist will come from the revived Roman Empire, and his people referred to here were the Romans who destroyed Jerusalem. It is significant that "war and its miseries are decreed from that time to the very end" (v.26 TLB). Surely no one doubts the constant fulfillment of this clause.

If you have ever wondered just what kind of a person the coming world dictator will be, then you should carefully study Daniel 9:27, in The Living Bible. Though we will look at this man later in detail, note that the verse says that he will: (1) make a seven-year treaty with the people; (2) after half that time, break his pledge and stop the Jews from all their sacrifices and offerings; (3) and then utterly defile the sanctuary of God.

His committing this abomination of desolation will signal the start of the latter half of the Tribulation, which Christ described as the most hideous times that ever existed (Matthew 24:21,22).

When Will the Prince Rule?

People who live for God are the deterrent to the coming of this world ruler. When we, the body of Christ, are taken from the world, then will this person, energized by Satan himself, come to world leadership. Paul discussed this dictator at length in his second letter to the Thessalonians:

For that day will not come until two things happen: first, there will be a time of great rebellion against God, and then the man of rebellion will come—the son of hell. He will defy every god there is, and tear down every other object of adoration and worship. He will go in and sit as God in the temple of God, claiming that he himself is God. As for the work this man of rebellion and hell will do when he comes, it is already going on, but he himself will not come until the one who is holding him back steps out of the way. (2 Thessalonians 2:3,4,7 TLB)

The one who is holding him back (v.7) apparently refers to the Holy Spirit that dwells in us, God's children, for ". . . your body is the temple of the Holy Ghost which is in you . . ." (1 Corinthians 6:19). We are that earth-salt that Jesus referred to in the Sermon on the Mount, and when we step out of the way, churlish imps of Satan will break loose upon the earth with their macabre works of death. The forces of hell will be headed up by the Antichrist, a mortal man right here on earth. Seemingly, he will be a European, emerging from the old Roman Empire (Daniel 7:8).

The Uncommon Market

On Thursday night, October 28, 1971, the British Parliament cast its historic majority vote favoring entrance into the European Common Market, effective January, 1973. Concerning that momentous event the *Mobile (Alabama) Press* carried a report the next day, which read: "The British decision to join the Common Market brought Western Europe to the threshold of its strongest union since the nations involved were tied together as part of the Roman Empire fifteen centuries ago. This time they were moving together by choice . . . building a free trade group that would rival the economic power of the United States or the Soviet Union."

The organization and development of the Common Market may be the link between today's events and the Tribulation, for the market may prove to be the actual revival of the old Roman Empire. From your world history studies you will remember that the Roman Empire was never defeated, but simply crumbled. The Bible seems to see that empire extending into the Tribulation period, and many Bible students believe that it will be revived as a ten-nation federation.

This is where the European Common Market enters the picture. An article carried in *Time* magazine a year or two ago said, ". . . the Common Market could someday expand into a ten-nation economic entity whose industrial might would far surpass that of the Soviet Union." Of course, the immediate intent of the market is to unite Europe economically, but the continent would probably unite militarily and politically also.

You may recall that Jean Monnet, the originator of the Market, stated, "As long as Europe remains divided, it is no match for the Soviet Union. Europe must unite." Though twenty or thirty years ago we could not imagine the possibility of a United States of Europe, today it is not only probable but is actually happening. This fact could well be signaling the immediacy of the return of Christ and the closeness of the Tribulation.

The Man With the Big Feet

Can you imagine a person having a most unusual dream, then forgetting what it was about, and later insisting upon threat of death that those about him recall the dream and tell him what it meant? The prophet Daniel was caught up in just such a bizarre situation when Nebuchadnezzar demanded that he and some others either recall and interpret his dream or die (Daniel 2). Typically, Daniel sought God about it and at night Jehovah revealed both the dream and the interpretation.

Daniel was shown that the king had seen a statue representing four world empires, and chapters 7 and 8 tell of Daniel's dream of correlating situations. The statue or image had a head of gold, representing the Babylonian Empire (likewise, the lion of chapter 7 represented that empire). The breast and arms of silver (and the bear of chapter 7 and the ram of chapter 8) foretold the Medo-Persian Empire. The belly and thighs of brass (and the leopard of chapter 7 and the he-goat of chapter 8) described the coming Grecian empire, while the legs of iron and ten toes of iron and clay (and the beast with ten horns of chapter 7; see also Revelation 17:12) represented the Roman Empire with its resultant ten nations. Of course, you know that the stone that was cut out of the mountain (see Daniel 2:45; also Revelation 11:15) is Christ Himself who will break to pieces the ten toes when He comes back to the earth following the Tribulation.

In studying this statue, you will note that it could not possibly stand forever, for it progressively weakens from head to toe, and its feet being iron mingled with clay give it a weak foundation, a foundation that Christ will crush with His "stone" kingdom that will last forever. This remarkable image is another of Daniel's incredible prophecies which, like his Seventy Weeks, foretells events right up to the time that Christ will return to earth to rule.

The Ten Toes

The Roman Empire was vast and for hundreds of years it wielded complete rule over much of the world. During her future revival era, the Scriptures seem to require that she expand even further (Revelation 13:7). As you realize, only the feet and toes portion of the image lacks fulfillment. These ten kingdoms do not have to fulfil only the area of the old Roman Empire, but are simply an outgrowth from the former stage of empire development.

Earlier it was stated that the emergence of the European Common Market may well be the beginning of the ten-nation federation represented by the ten toes of Daniel's prophecy. Of course, we do not know this for certain. The market could fall apart and then overnight another federation could be formed, fulfilling Daniel's prophecy. However, we do know that the ten-nation block will be in existence when Christ returns to the earth, for He will crush it. The Common Market certainly has the appearance of the rise of the ten-nation confederacy, and those nations comprising it are in the same general area of the old Roman Empire.

Did you notice in Daniel's prophecy of the ten toes or nations, that he says they will be gored by a "little horn" (7:8)? This horn, a person, apparently will rule the entire world (Revelation 13:7), and he will be a remarkable individual indeed. The Bible has a good deal to say about him, calling him by different names. John called him "the beast" (Revelation 13:4), Paul, "that man of sin" (2 Thessalonians 2:3), and again, John called him "antichrist" (1 John 4:3). Other writers gave him other names. The Apocalypse points out that the ten-toe federation ruled over by this world dictator will be short-lived (Revelation 13:5; 17:10).

A World Government?

Though it is difficult to comprehend nations relinquishing their sovereignty in deference to a world government, it does appear more of a possibility now than a few years ago. We now have a world court, a world bank, a world council of churches, and some people are wanting a world government, even to the point of having already prepared a provisional constitution. During a Vatican Council, Cardinal Alfredo Ottaviani received the heartiest response ever given there when he urged that the council call upon governments to join in a single world republic to preserve peace.

Not knowing the Bible's predictions of a universal government under the Satan-dominated Antichrist, many people feel that the United Nations or some stronger form of world government is the only hope for the world. Arnold Toynbee, the renowned historian, said on a radio broadcast, ". . . technology has brought mankind to such a degree of distress that we are ripe for the deifying of any Caesar who might succeed in giving the world unity and peace." The Antichrist, whom the Bible calls the "man of sin" (2 Thessalonians 2:3), will probably bring unity and peace, though it will not last, for the Tribulation will be plagued with wars (Matthew 24:6,7).

A Close Look at Antichrist

You will remember from history that Hitler stepped upon the scene at an opportune time. Germany was out of work, out of money, and desperate. Many saw in Hitler a way out, and he saw in himself a hero, a strong man needed by the weak, a person above the law, free to act as he saw fit. So the madman took the reins of Germany and went a long way toward conquering the world.

On a much grander scale than Hitler, the Antichrist will quickly assume world leadership, probably by either force or a coup. Other than Christ, he will be the greatest personality ever to appear upon earth. *He will be a genius.* Daniel says he will have "eyes like the eyes of man" (7:8; see also Revelation 4:6) denoting intelligence. Displaying remarkable ability before the ten kings, he will be given full power (Revelation 17:13). Bible students believe that his number, 666 (Revelation 13:18), denotes perfection closest to divinity that an unregenerate man can attain as it relates to intelligence, personality, and ability. Even Satan will recognize his genius and will give to him "his power, and his seat, and great authority" (Revelation 13:2). Moreover, he will have the acumen to pull to himself the remarkable false prophet, a person who will double as his premier and his press secretary (Revelation 13:11–17).

He will be a politician. Daniel says that ". . . through his policy also he shall cause craft to prosper in his hand" (8:25). People will feel secure with him in leadership and he will craftily use them for his own ends. Being willing to stoop to any level in order to fully secure his world dominion, he will submit to the apostate church (Revelation 17:3,7), but when he is through with that religious system he will destroy it (Revelation 17:16,17).

As you can imagine, mankind has discussed this coming world ruler for years. Just after the turn of the century *Harper's* magazine carried a verbal portrait of him. In 1902 its editors stated: "There will arise 'the man.' He will be strong in action, epigrammatic in manner, personally handsome, and continuously victorious. He will sweep aside parliaments and demagogues, carry civilizations to glory, reconstruct them into an empire, and hold it together by circulating his profile and organizing further successes. He will codify everything, galvanize Christianity; he will organize learning into meek academies of little men and prescribe a wonderful educational system, and the grateful nations will deify a lucky and progressive egotism."

He will have personal charm. The Antichrist will be looked upon as a superman, and the world will worship him. His phenomenal rise to power, his military genius, and his exploits, will be nothing short of spectacular and colossal. Further, he will be a public speaker par excellence and will sway the world with his "mouth speaking great things" (Daniel 7:8). John says he will have a "mouth of a lion" (Revelation 13:2), probably suggesting strength and authority in what he says.

If you will read other apocalyptic passages about his words, you will note that much of his speech is against God, or the Lord Jesus, or the saints. For example: "And there was given unto him a mouth speaking . . . blasphemies" (13:5); "And he opened his mouth in blasphemy against God, to blaspheme his name, and his tabernacle, and them that dwell in heaven" (13:-6).

What Will Life Be Like Then?

Today's sophisticated man is prone to make the Tribulation so far removed from himself that it has an "another world" appearance. However, such will not actually be the case. The Tribulation will take place right here upon this earth, probably among people living today, for it could start any time. After the Rapture the Tribulation will begin, and though it is to last only seven years, there will probably be a gradual transition, into the dark days to follow.

Man will continue to advance scientifically. Planned technological advances on the drawing boards today may be developed then if they are not done earlier. For example, there is talk of development of a sugar-cube-size apparatus that would store as much information as contained in the Library of Congress. The student, the businessman, or the housewife would pull the cube from his pocket or purse, decode the desired information electronically, and quickly find desired facts. Also, science may develop moons which would be sun-reflecting satellites in space and turn all nights into twilight.

Further, there are plans for television screens which would hang flat against the walls like pictures. During the Tribulation cars will be bought and sold, roads will be built, and crops will be planted and harvested. In general, life will continue to some degree as usual for awhile except that the world will be much more materialistic, and much less spiritual, for the true Church will not be here.

This is not to say that life will be easy then, for it will be the opposite. Satan will rule the world and the crime rate will probably skyrocket. Morals will drop even lower than they are now, and God will be publically attacked (Revelation 13:6). Besides, the judgments of God will be poured out upon the earth.

Worship During the Tribulation.

Someone has said that at least 90 percent of what we do in our churches today could be carried on as usual, should the Holy Spirit be taken away. What an indictment against true worship! However, one can imagine a good deal of today's public worship going on as usual the Sunday following the Rapture. Many people today give only lip service to Christ. Other professing Christians deny numerous facets of the faith, such as the virgin birth of Christ, the regeneration which Jesus offers, the return of Christ in the Rapture, and the inspiration of His holy Word.

Some people simply go to church because their heart, which has not been surrendered to Christ, longs for fellowship with God, and church attendance somehow appeases that yearning. Yet, they have never repented of their sins and accepted Christ into their lives. They may have religion, morality, and know some theology, but they have never been made a new creature in Christ. Since Christ is not returning just for good people, but for men, women, boys and girls who truly know Him, He will leave all unregenerate people here. Many of those left would go to church the following Sunday, probably with renewed interest in the spiritual side of life.

The Coming World Church

Have you ever wondered about the plain language used in Revelation 17 where it speaks of a harlot? That disreputable woman is God's way of describing, by use of symbolic language, the world religion during the first half of the Tribulation. Even today there is a strong move in many quarters to amalgamate all denominations into a super world church. Dr. Henry P. Van Dusen has said, "To an age destined to survive, if at all, as 'one world,' we bring the beginnings of a united church." Dr. J. V. Langmead-Casserly, an Episcopal theologian, has predicted that by the turn of the century there will be "a great united church under the leadership of a reinterpreted papacy."

Concerning the coming world church, Charles H. Stevens, writing in the book *Prophecy and the Seventies,* predicted: "There will be the establishment of one world religion . . . on the concept of the universal Fatherhood of God and brotherhood of man."

The world church, being completely apostatized, will be altogether divorced from the principles of faith held today by the Christian Church. The Bible refers to this world religion symbolically as Babylon, and that city is mentioned more in the Scriptures than any other city except Jerusalem, being referred to more than 260 times. For years a world church has been discussed.

For example, it was considered in 1910 during the World Conference on Missionary Cooperation at Edinburgh. Many of the church leaders involved in today's World Council of Churches are liberalistic, and liberalism has long denied the deity of Christ and His Second Coming.

You may have noticed a newspaper article a few months ago which quoted Gus Hall, the infamous Communist Party leader in America, as saying that the Communist goals for America are almost identical to those projected by the liberal church leaders of our nation. When such godless men as Hall can align with religion, that religion needs to be watched!

Just as the ecumenical church of today appears to be laying the foundation for the apostate church of the Tribulation, so communism has laid the groundwork for the form of atheism that will result in a world religion when God will be completely forsaken and man will worship Satan in the person of the

Antichrist during the latter half of the Tribulation (Revelation 13:4). Today we have people holding meetings in America for the express purpose of worshiping Satan. Further, Satan uses witchcraft and mind-expanding drugs, among other things, to pull attention to himself. Some habitual users of drugs will tell you that they know there is a devil, for they have seen him. A contemporary so-called witch said, "We worship a horned god, the prince of darkness, and this makes some people say we are devil-worshipers." All of these things are forerunners of the atheistic type of worship that will be the state religion during the Tribulation (Revelation 13:15).

End of the World Religion

As you can well imagine, the church structure remaining after the Rapture will be without the people of God. Its ministry will not know God, and its theology will ignore God's Word. Such an organization is destined to suffer the judgment of the Almighty. The Bible presents this apostate church symbolically as a harlot, a wicked woman, riding a scarlet beast (Revelation 13). Though the beast (the Antichrist) is the world ruler (Revelation 13), the church is riding him, signifying the power of the church.

Apparently, the apostate church and the Antichrist will make an alliance and will ride into complete world power together. The Antichrist desires to be worshiped, and when he no longer needs the apostate church, he will destroy it (Revelation 17:16). In fact, God leads him to do so (v.17).

Then the Antichrist will set up his own worship system (note how often the word *worship* is used in Revelation 13), and during the last three and a half years of the Tribulation Satan worship will be the state religion. In fact, this seems to be the reason for taking the mark of the beast, for the mark "in their right hand, or in their foreheads" (13:16) will probably give testimony that the people acknowledge the Antichrist as God. The Scriptures state further, "as many as would not worship the image of the beast should be killed" (v.15). May God deliver us from such demon-possessed times!

Are People Converted During the Tribulation?

In his book *The Bible and Tomorrow's News,* Charles C. Ryrie believes that the six seal judgments of God (Revelation 6:1–17) will probably take place upon earth during the first year of the Tribulation, the first seal (conquest) in the first few months. He thinks the second seal (war) and the third (famine) will closely follow. Incidentally Ryrie, along with some other scholars, thinks that the seven-year Tribulation does not necessarily start the day after the Rapture. He says there may be a time lapse, pointing out that not the Rapture, but the Antichrist's making a seven-year pact with Israel (Daniel 9:27), marks the beginning of that holocaust.

During this time of God's judgment upon a Satan-controlled world, people will be converted. A group of 144,000 zealous evangelists who themselves will have turned to God after the Rapture (Revelation 7:4), will proclaim God's righteousness. The ecumenical world church will oppose this strong witness, and will, in the name of religion, kill people for their faith. The Bible says the church will be "drunken with the blood of the saints, and with the blood of the martyrs of Jesus" (Revelation 17:6).

Hal Lindsey says that the 144,000 will evangelize with the zeal of Billy Graham. Think of evangelists scattering throughout the world proclaiming the redeeming grace of God. The

Bible gives the results of their labor: "After this I beheld, and, lo, a great multitude, which no man could number, of all nations, and kindreds, and people, and tongues, stood before the throne, and before the Lamb, clothed with white robes, and palms in their hands. . . . These are they which came out of great tribulation, and have washed their robes, and made them white in the blood of the Lamb" (Revelation 7:9, 14).

You will note that this reference testifies to two facts: (1) many, many people will turn to the Lord during the Tribulation, and (2) thousands upon thousands will be slaughtered because of their faith.

The Two Witnesses

The Two Witnesses of Revelation 11 stand out like the rock of Gibraltar in the turbulent sea of world conflict. You will find the Holy Spirit's account of them as follows: "These two have the power to shut up the sky, so that no rain may fall during the time of their prophesying; and they have the power to turn water to blood and to strike the earth at will with every kind of plague. But when they have completed their testimony, the beast that comes up from the abyss will wage war upon them and will defeat and kill them" (Revelation 11:6,7 NEB).

Though some students believe these two men will live during the latter half of the Tribulation, scholars such as Pentecost, Walvoord, Biederwolf and others place them in the first. It seems that they will appear before the "abomination of desolation" (Matthew 24:15) which will take place in the middle of the Tribulation. Some think that Antichrist will slay the witnesses, destroy the apostate church, and break his covenant with Israel rapidly and in that order. But until God permits it, he can do nothing with the two unusual witnesses.

Like the Old Testament prophets who called down fire, they will have power to kill their adversaries with fire. Further, they will turn water to blood, bring plagues, and prevent rain. These two saints will cause no little annoyance to the Antichrist and his cohorts when they decide to invoke a worldwide drought, causing great devastation, along with the other disasters visiting the earth.

Who Are They?

Many and varied have been the opinions of students concerning the identity of these witnesses, including Moses and Elijah or Enoch and Elijah. However, others feel that you cannot know who they will be. W. A. Criswell, writing in his *Expository Sermons on Revelations,* volume 4, said: "I have one suggestion to make about their identification and it is this: from every syllable that is written here in the Word, I would think they are men, they are persons. . . . We do not know who they are. We shall have to wait and see."

The World Sees a Wonder

You will note that "when they have completed their testimony," Antichrist slays the Two Witnesses. The great problems they cause this world ruler is indicated by his vindictive actions after their death. We do not know what weapon is used to murder the witnesses, but once they are killed ". . . their dead bodies shall lie in the streets . . . of the great city . . . three days and a half . . ." (Revelation 11:8), and Antichrist will not allow them to be buried! Apparently these two preachers will have been a great annoyance to many people. Antichrist will probably declare a holiday, and the people will rejoice, and send each other gifts—the only incident of joy in the otherwise somber seven-year period.

As long as the witnesses' bodies lie in the street, the whole world will look upon them at will (v.9) thanks to television and satellites. Feeling that they had destroyed the last vestige of righteousness, you can imagine some making quick trans-oceanic flights to Jerusalem to see the bodies and to celebrate. If they had believed the preaching of the witnesses, they would be sad and would not be rejoicing.

However, you can well imagine the worldwide dismay when in the middle of the fourth day ". . . the spirit of life from God entered into them, and they stood upon their feet . . ." (v.11). Think of it! While the world watches, two decaying bodies come to life, stand up, and ascend to heaven in answer to a "great voice," which millions may also hear via microphones and television. Imagine all of this happening in a day of Satan worship and almost total denial of God. This is not all that transpires that day. An earthquake centered in Jerusalem will kill thousands of individuals. Then people will be afraid ". . . and gave glory to the God of heaven" (v.13).

The Other Half

After Antichrist kills the two witnesses, he will destroy the apostate church as has been mentioned earlier, and forfeit his seven-year contract with the Jews. Then will break lose the last three and a half years of the period, the time Christ called the Great Tribulation. A world war will develop and armies will gather for the great battle of Armageddon, which Christ will end with His triumphant return to earth. Those events we will discuss in a later chapter. The discussion in this chapter about the first three and one half years of the Tribulation is not at all intended to be exhaustive, but rather an overview of that period with a close look at some of the events prophesied. With the two witnesses in mind and all the others through the centuries who have given their lives for their faith, I end this chapter with the following poem:

> I saw the martyrs at the stake,
> The flames could not his courage shake,
> Nor death his soul appall.
> I ask him whence his strength was given,
> He looked triumphantly to heaven
> And answered, "Christ is all."

5

The Red Sunset

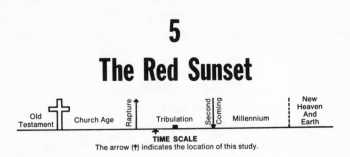

TIME SCALE
The arrow (†) indicates the location of this study.

More than twenty-five hundred years ago the Biblical prophet Ezekiel predicted the fall of Russia. He gave a fantastic prophecy about a military confrontation which you probably have not heard nearly so much about as you have of the campaign of Armageddon. However, the military advancement of Russia into Palestine and her complete destruction by God on the hillsides of Israel is just as supernatural as the outcome of Armageddon.

The holy Scriptures even locate and name the vast new cemetery that will develop solely as a place of burial of the Red army. So many Russians will die that it will take the Israelis seven months to bury them. The stench of decaying men will cause Palestineans to hold their noses when they pass by. You could well ask on what basis are such incredible statements made. Does such talk come from a world premier mystery movie or a futuristic horror paperback? No, these predictions are in God's holy Word!

At this point you should go to your Bible and carefully read chapters 38 and 39 of Ezekiel, which talk about a country named *Rosh,* and her subsequent destruction. The King James

Version does not name *Rosh* in 38:2, but others, such as the New English Bible and the Amplified Bible, do. These two chapters state that Rosh (Russia) and her allies will invade Israel when that little country is "at rest" (38:11) to "take a spoil" (v. 13). When the Reds get into the land, they "shalt fall upon the mountains of Israel, thou, and all thy bands, and the people that is with thee" (39:4); that is, Russia's allies.

Is Rosh Russia?

First, we should substantiate the fact that Biblical Rosh was in reality modern Russia. You will notice that in Ezekiel 38:2 the prophet was told, ". . . set your face against Gog, of the land of Magog, the prince of Rosh, of Meshech, and Tubal . . ." (AMPLIFIED). Many Bible scholars agree that ancient Rosh was what is now Russia, and some think that Meshech is Moscow and Tubal is modern Tobolsk. Such contemporary Bible scholars as Dwight Pentecost, Clarence Mason, Jr., Wilbur Smith, Lehman Strauss, George Britt and many others concur that Biblical Rosh is Russia. Wilbur Smith commented recently in *Decision* magazine, "Now, 'Rosh' in the Greek text . . . is certainly Russia; there is no question about it."

Long before Russia became a world power, Bible students realized that God's Word spoke of that country. In his book *The Prophet Ezekiel,* in 1918, Arno C. Gaebelein stated: "Careful research has established the fact that . . . Rosh is Russia. . . . The prince of Rosh means, therefore, the prince or king of the Russian Empire." At the recent Diamond Jubilee Congress on Prophecy convening in New York, Dr. Clarence E. Mason, Jr., commented, "The name 'Rosh' would be a typically variant spelling of Russia, and in his definitive work entitled *Things to Come,* Dr. Dwight Pentecost reckoned, ". . . the identification of Rosh as modern Russia would seem to be well authenticated and generally accepted."

I will not tax you with endless comments of scholars, but I should mention that the first-century Jewish historian, Flavis Josephus said, "Magog (who was a grandson of Noah) founded those that from him were named Magogites, but who by the Greeks were called Sythians." Scholars say that the Russians came from the Sythians.

Go North, Young Man

It is believed that after the Flood some of the grandsons of Noah migrated northward beyond the Caspian and Black Seas and ultimately settled in what is now Russia. Therefore Gomer, Magog, Tubal and Meshech, who are named in Genesis, chapter 10, as the sons of Japeth, the son of Noah, turn up in Ezekiel as names of places "in the uttermost parts of the north" (38:6 AMPLIFIED).

Should you lay a ruler on a map showing both Palestine and Russia, you would note that Russia is directly north of Israel, and you would find that the Soviet Union reaches utterly as far as land extends into the frigid arctic circle. Russia is a vast northern country spreading six thousand miles east to west and three thousand miles north to south. Also, Moscow is nearly fifteen hundred miles due north of Jerusalem.

A Land That Prosperity Visited

Almost six hundred years before Christ, Ezekiel said that Russia would someday begin to prosper, for he related "After many days thou shalt be visited . . ." (38:8). Evidently the prophet meant that the country would begin to prosper both economically and politically. None of us doubt that this reference has been fulfilled, for today that super world power is very strong, wielding influence throughout the world. Not only is she today a military threat to Palestine as the Scriptures predicted, but she is a threat to the peace of the world as well.

Have you considered that Ezekiel's prophecy of Russia invading Israel could not have possibly taken place until the last few years? This is true for two reasons: (1) Russia was not strong enough to launch such an attack and withstand subsequent world repercussions; (2) More important, there was no country of Israel in existence for her to attack until the last quarter-century. Incidentally, you will notice that this is another definite indication of our living in the closing years of this age. The prophet said that Russian invasion would come "in the latter years" (38:8).

Moshe Dayan, Israel's ingenious defense minister, has said that "the next war will not be with the Arabs but with the Russians." In a television interview some months ago Rabbi Ruben Slonim stated that the Russians are putting much more money into the Arab world than in all of their other schemes put together.

As you have observed, Ezekiel told us why Russia, the superpower, would invade the very small country of Israel. "To take a spoil, and to take a prey" (38:12) will be the purpose. Providence has seen to it that Israel has an unbelievable wealth of natural deposits. Just recently there was an important oil and gas discovery south of the Dead Sea. The mineral reserves in the Dead Sea area may well have a potential value equal to the combined wealth of France, England, and the United States. Those mineral deposits include a fantastic amount of potash, bromide, salt, gypsum, calcium chloride and magnesium chloride.

As you can understand, aggressive Russia will not be willing to leave the ripe plum of little Israel untouched. Even today she could have Israel's conquest in mind as she continues to make deeper and deeper inroads into the Middle East. A recent issue of the *U.S. News and World Report* stated: "Nowhere have the Russians made greater gains since the Cuban missile crisis than in the Middle East—and nowhere have they taken greater risks."

The Reds Hate Israel

The gospel of the communists is the antithesis of that of the Hebrews, for while the former preaches a no-God, no-heaven, no-morals doctrine, such tenets as God, heaven and high morals are at the very heart of Judaism. This must be why Ezekiel observed that the Soviets would go to Israel ". . . to turn thine hand upon the desolate places that are now inhabited, and upon the people that are gathered out of the nations . . ." (38:12). Russia hates Israel, which is evidenced by her massive slaughter of six million Jews since just before the turn of the century until today.

As you have found in your study of history, communism took over Russia in October-November, 1917, and immediately a statement was released which read, "No church or religious association shall enjoy the rights of judicial persons." What this said in practice was that synagogue and church worship, Sunday school, or any other kind of religious meeting was illegal and was forbidden to exist. In his excellent work *Russian Events in the Light of Prophecy,* Louis Bauman points out that Sunday schools or any other schools for religious guidance were positively not tolerated. He says that throughout the vast nation of Russia it became a criminal offense for a mother to teach her child a verse of the Bible. As you are well aware, Russia and all other communistic countries still firmly hold an anti-God, anti-Bible rule.

An Enigma Wrapped In A Paradox

As you know too well, communism is not restricted to one nation, for it crosses borders to the point that today it enslaves nearly half the world. Communism is a philosophy, an anti-God religion, an ideology to which the Soviets have given strong impetus. Theirs is an impish kind of philosophy, which, voiced by Lenin, says, "Treaties are only for getting breath for a new effort. They exist to be broken as soon as expedient. Peace propaganda is to camouflage war preparations."

There is little wonder that Moscow's communists have baffled world political leaders for a generation. Winston Churchill lamented, "I cannot forecast to you the action of Russia. It is a riddle, wrapped in a mystery, inside an enigma." Neither can you nor I forecast the day-to-day action of Russia, but we can know where and how that nation will end, for Ezekiel carefully spells that out.

The Russians Are Coming

The Soviets and their allies will someday invade Israel, and you can well imagine the suspense and awe that will sweep the world when Russia and her throng stand eye-to-eye with Antichrist and his forces. The prophet describes the invasion: "Thou shalt ascend and come like a storm, thou shalt be like a cloud to cover the land, thou and all thy bands, and many people with thee . . . thou shalt say . . . I will go to them that are at rest . . . it shall be in the latter days . . ." (Ezekiel 38:9, 11, 12, 16).

You noticed that Ezekiel made two points as to when the

Reds will invade: (1) When Israel is at rest, and (2) in the last days. Israel is certainly not at rest now, but rather, she is buffeted from all sides. Recently Anwar Sadat of Egypt said that another war with Israel is inevitable, and it is apparent that the Israelis are concerned. Prime Minister Golda Meir was in the United States recently trying to persuade President Nixon to sell fighter planes to her country, stating that they desperately need them for survival. No, Israel is not now at rest, but is constantly threatened, and since the Reds will attack when she is resting peacefully, the invasion will have to come later, generally believed to be during the first three and a half years of the Tribulation.

Dr. John F. Walvoord, president of Dallas Theological Seminary, wrote in *The Prophetic Word in Crisis Days:* "There is only one period in the future that clearly fits this description of Ezekiel, and that is the first half of Daniel's seventieth week of God's program for Israel" (Daniel 9:27). Ezekiel also said that the Reds would come "in the latter days." Bible students concur that we are now living the period which the Bible calls the last days, but the period is an extended span of time lasting until the end of the Tribulation. Therefore, the Russian invasion will be during "the last hours" of the last days.

The Rapture—Then the Russians

I stood at Jerusalem's Wailing Wall a few months ago and was deeply moved as I observed Jews praying aloud while others read from their Scriptures. Standing facing the wall, the weather-beaten joints of which were dotted with paper containing written prayers of earlier visitors, these earnest people were imploring God in the Hebrew tongue. It was easy to imagine that some of their prayers had to do with petitions for the soon coming of their Messiah. Though you and I know that He has come, they have not accepted the fact, hence, they pray on.

When the Lord Jesus returns to the earth after the Tribulation, then the Jews will accept Him as the Messiah. Zechariah describes that moving scene: " 'Then I will pour out the spirit of grace and prayer on all the people of Jerusalem, and they will look on him they pierced, and mourn for him as for an only son, and grieve bitterly for him as for an oldest child who died' " (12:10 TLB).

However, the godliest of the Jews who have not accepted Christ will not go in the Rapture, for Christ comes at that time only for those who are part of His Church. As you understand, then, most of the Jews will be left upon the earth when the Church is raptured. Actually, the Tribulation will serve to turn many Jews to Christ. It is believed that God's intervention for Israel against Russia will be the reason for many of the Israelis turning completely to God and His Son, who will be preached regularly by the 144,000 evangelists.

The Time Seems Near

When you remember that today Russia is giving more attention to the Middle East than ever before, and the Israelis are saying that their next war will be with Russia, you quickly see how Ezekiel's prophecy could be fulfilled soon. We may be approaching the ultimate end of this age. Of course, we do not know when Christ will return, but Biblical prophecies of events following the Rapture seem to be in sight. Shadows of the horrible Tribulation fall long across our way. Therefore, Christ could return at any moment, then Antichrist would take world command, and after about three and a half years Russia would march against Palestine and would be wiped out there.

Their Sun Will Set, Too

The total strength of the nations that will march against Israel is herculean. The Bible spells out those countries (Ezekiel 38:5, 6), and the writer infers that even more than those named will be involved, for after naming Russia's allies, he adds, "and many people with thee." Apparently, the Soviets will need all this support if they are to hope to overcome Antichrist and his armies, who will be protecting Israel. Note the names of the countries allied with Russia: "Persia, Ethiopia, and Libya with them; all of them with shield and helmet: Gomer, and all his bands; the house of Togarmah of the north quarters, and all his bands: and many people with thee" (Ezekiel 38:5, 6).

It is generally conceded that Persia is modern Iran, and it is significant that recently the Soviet Union has moved to more closely ally itself with that country. Russia would need to cross Iran on its way to Palestine, for that route would be the easiest. Biblical Ethiopia was larger than today's country by that name, for it is believed to have included all the black nations of Africa. When you notice the foothold that Russia now has in Africa, you can understand how someday they could march with Russia to war.

Libya, originally Put (the name derives from Put, a son of Ham, the son of Noah) takes in what is now the Arab nations of North Africa, and here again we know that Soviet communism is ever broadening its stance in these countries, including Libya, Algeria, Tunisia, and Morocco.

The End of Eastern Europe

Ezekiel said that Gomer would be among Russia's northern allies. In Genesis 10 Gomer was a son of Japheth, the son of

Noah, and as has been pointed out earlier, these grandsons of Noah migrated northward. Scholars state that Gomer is now Germany, especially East Germany. In ancient times it was much larger and included what is now that vast area of Eastern Europe that is held by the communists. Hence, you can well see how Gomer would be Russia's ally.

Also, the prophet mentioned Togarmah, and as with the other places named in his prophecy, this one too can be identified today. Ancient Togarmah was part of what is today southern Russia. Hence, the Holy Spirit through Ezekiel carefully catalogs most of Russia's allies that will march with her as she invades Israel. The Bible indicates that Russia's allies will die on the hillsides of Palestine.

When the Reds Come to Israel

Not only does Ezekiel spend two chapters discussing the invasion and subsequent destruction of Russia and her confederacy, but Daniel also speaks of that event: "And at the time of the end . . . the king of the north shall come against him like a whirlwind, with chariots, and with horsemen, and with many ships; and he shall enter into the countries, and shall overflow and pass over. He shall enter also into the glorious land [Palestine]" (Daniel 11:40, 41).

Note how explicit the prophet is. He states that "at the time of the end . . . the king of the north [Russia and her allies] shall come against him [the Antichrist] like a whirlwind." Daniel says this will happen at the end of the age, and even now those coming events seem to be looming on the horizon, casting their shadows on our times. Since Russia will oppose Antichrist when she invades the Holy Land, it is evident that Antichrist will still be keeping his contract to protect Israel, which he will later break by committing the "abomination of desolation" (Matthew 24).

Not only does Russia prepare to launch a land attack "with chariots, and with horsemen," but also she is poised for attack from the Mediterranean Sea "with many ships," aircraft carriers and probably submarines. Hundreds of thousands of soldiers will "enter also into the glorious land" carrying many, many tons of supplies and equipment.

The Lord Fights the Reds

Just as the Reds are poised to deal a colossal and devastating blow against little Palestine, supernatural, unexplainable things begin to happen against them, and in their consternation the Reds even turn and begin to fight each other, reminiscent of the confusion of the Midianites hundreds of years earlier (Judges 7:22). Commenting on those times in *When Dust Shall Sing,* George Britt observed, "The Russian giant is poised to strike, and according to the immutable Word the supreme effort will not be in Europe or the Far East, or over the North Pole. The Russian might will be humbled and slain in Israel's land, and will be buried in a valley in Israel which from henceforth will be known as Hamongog."

Ezekiel describes the providential intervention against Russia as follows: "Surely in that day there shall be a great shaking in the land of Israel . . . every man's sword shall be against his brother. And I will plead against him [Russia] with pestilence and with blood; and I will rain upon him, and upon his bands, and upon the many people that are with him, an overflowing rain, and great hailstones, fire, and brimstone. Thus will I magnify myself . . . and I will be known in the eyes of many nations, and they shall know that I am the Lord" (38:19–23).

Joel Speaks of the Army

"I will remove far off from you the northern army, and will drive him into a land barren and desolate, with his face toward the east sea, and his hinder part toward the utmost sea, and his stink shall come up, and his ill savour shall come up, because he hath done great things" (2:20). The "east sea" is the Dead Sea and the "utmost sea" the Mediterranean. If Joel means that this army will reach all the way from one sea to the other, that is about fifty miles, illustrating the massiveness of the Red army.

A footnote in The Amplified Bible refers to the army's size and doom: "The number of dead bodies left, after the great catastrophe which God will send upon Gog and his hosts, as here described, would necessarily amount to several millions . . . not some, but "all" of God's multitude will die then (Ezekiel 39:4, 11). That one-sixth of the horde from the north will be left alive, as the King James Version says (39:2), is without noted exception conceded to be a mistaken translation by all authorities of modern times."

When Israel Holds Its Nose

Can you imagine how foul the air will be when millions of human bodies begin to decay? The Bible takes time to tell us about it. Joel says, "And its stench shall come up . . . and its foul odor shall come up" (2:20 AMPLIFIED), while Ezekiel comments, "it shall stop the noses of the passengers" (39:11). After these millions ". . . fall [dead] upon the mountains of Israel" (39:4 AMPLIFIED), the Israelis will set aside a massive cemetery

over by the Dead Sea and will name it the Valley of Hamongog
(v. 11).

Collecting and bringing bodies to the Valley of Hamongog
burial grounds will be a national ecological project. For seven
months "all the people of the land shall bury them" (v. 13), and
after that "they shall sever out men of continual employment"
(v.14) to bury those that remain. Whenever a skeleton is found,
a marker will be placed by it, so that the burying crew may find
it and take it to the graveyard near the Dead Sea. Thus the
people will cleanse the land.

When the destruction is over and the dead are buried, God
Himself states the lasting results: "And I will set my glory
among the heathen [surely, none are more heathenish than the
communists], and all the heathen shall see my judgment that
I have executed, and my hand that I have laid upon them. So
the house of Israel shall know that I am the Lord their God
from that day forward" (Ezekiel 39:21,22). It appears that this
great intervention of God for Israel will cause many to believe
in their true Messiah.

What About the Future?

This study brings to the front several important facts. For
one thing, Russia apparently will never rule the world; she is
not one of the four world empires foretold in the second chapter
of Daniel. Instead of Russia ultimately conquering the other
superpowers of the globe, she will meet her humiliating end in
the little nation of Israel.

The second very obvious conclusion is that developments
described in the Bible at the time of the end are already on the
scene. As you are aware, Russia is in the Middle East, Israel
is in Palestine, and the Arabs, backed by the Soviets, are threat-

ening to annihilate Israel. It is as though the stage is set and the world is waiting for the curtain to go up on the last act of Gentile domination, headed up by Antichrist.

Third, it is evident that all things are now ready for the return of Christ to take away all the believers of the world. It seems conclusive that He must return before Russia can invade Palestine; in fact, all that is lacking to start completion of this age is for Christ to return so that the Antichrist can set up his rule, bringing peace to Israel, so that Russia can invade the little country.

Fourth, there is another fact that weighs heavily on my heart, and that is your preparation for the future. Throughout the foregoing pages I have assumed that you are a believer, and would, therefore, not be around when the events discussed in this chapter take place. Am I mistaken? Is it possible that you have not repented of your sins and been made anew in Christ? If so, it may be that Christ is delaying His return so that you might come to Him. Note what Peter says: "He isn't really being slow about his promised return, even though it sometimes seems that way. But he is waiting, for the good reason that he is not willing that any should perish, and he is giving more time for sinners to repent" (2 Peter 3:9 TLB).

Christ could have come last year, but He did not, and thousands are rejoicing today in the knowledge that they have found Him within the last few months. If you are not a believer, you should turn to Him today, for things are now ready for the Lord's return, and this may be the last year He will wait in order for you to turn to Him.

6

Shalom

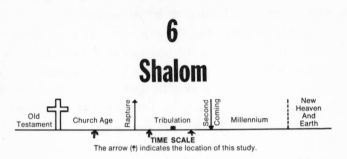

The arrow (†) indicates the location of this study.

According to prophetic Scripture, God intends to bring about a thousand years of peace with a Jewish Messiah as the Ruler, Jersulaem as the world capital, Israel as the chosen land, and the rest of the world under the peaceful dominion of the righteous Messiah. God's plans for the Jews and the Holy Land are everlasting. History began in the Middle East, and that same geographical area will someday be the center of the world's activities. Throughout eternity the Jews will play an important part in God's economy. Even the twelve gates to the New Jerusalem will each bear the name of Jacob's sons (Revelation 21:12).

God's Measuring Stick

Among all the peoples of the earth, none are as remarkable as the Jews. They are God's measuring stick, the road map that guides us so that we may know and understand the future. God focuses on the Jew, and as someone has well said, "As goes the Jew, so goes the world." This is true, even though down through the centuries the Jews have been discriminated against,

90

ostracized, tortured, sold into slavery, and massacred by the millions. Anti-Semitism is ever part of their lot, and one of the marvels of history is that they have survived as a race and are now reuniting in Israel.

As you study the Bible you will find that not only do the Jewish people and the land of Palestine figure prominently in things to come, but so does the city of Jerusalem. That ancient place is destined to become the economic, social, and religious center of the world. God's chosen people are back in that city and they are determined to hold onto it. You may have read in the newspapers recently of the speech in Los Angeles by Israeli Foreign Minister Abba Eban. He asserted that his country is back to stay in all of Jerusalem. "Will Israel withdraw?" Eban queried, as he repeated a reporter's question concerning Israel's occupying Old Jerusalem since 1967. He answered, "Will France withdraw from Paris? Will England withdraw from London?" Nor will Israel withdraw, he asserted, pointing out that all of Jerusalem is a part of Israel, and withdrawal is out of the question.

Shalom Means Peace

Throughout the length and breadth of Israel the oft-repeated greeting is shalom (pronounced sha-loam). Used for hello, good morning, hi, and even good-bye, shalom is constantly on the lips of the people. The use of the term is prophetic, for someday genuine peace will reign there. When the Prince of Peace, the Messiah, comes to Jerusalem, peace will spread throughout the earth from that old city.

On the first day that Old Jerusalem was joined to the new part of the city after the Six-Day War (1967), people were excited and joyful. In Jerusalem the Reverend W. Z. Kofsmann pastors the Assembly of God Church, which is the largest Hebrew Christian congregation in Israel. Pastor Kofsmann described the first day of a united Jerusalem in a letter to Arnold Olson, which Olson printed in his book *Inside Jerusalem.* Kofsmann said, "Everywhere one could hear, 'Shalom, shalom! Peace, peace!' This greeting is becoming more and more a hope and a prayer. The time of peace is near, for the Almighty has promised it: 'And in this place will I give peace, saith the Lord of Hosts' (Haggai 2:9). From here peace will spread over the whole earth."

The aging David Ben-Gurion, the first premier of modern Israel, talked of peace while addressing the delegates at the Jerusalem Conference on Biblical Prophecy in June, 1971. He commented, "Probably not in my lifetime, but in yours, Isaiah's prophecy of peace, that the people shall no longer learn of war, will come true." It is significant that the intrepid old statesman was referring to Isaiah's prophecy of the day when Christ will carry out His worldwide peaceful reign from Jerusalem (Isaiah 2:1-4).

God's Chosen People

You have probably wondered about the Jewish people. Why is God so explicit concerning that race belonging to Him? Does He love the Jews more than the other races which are also part of His creation? God's Word gives a clear answer to this question in the call to Abraham thousands of years ago. It reads: "And I will make of thee a great nation, and I will bless thee, and make thy name great; and thou shall be a blessing: And I will bless them that bless thee, and curse him that curseth thee: and in thee shall all families of the earth be blessed" (Genesis 12:2,3).

There you have the answer. God elected and commissioned the Jews so that they in turn would be a spiritual blessing to the rest of the world. Ultimately "all the families of the earth" would be blessed through the Messiah who would redeem all families and reign over them in peace.

Commenting on God's selection of Abraham and through him the selection of the Jews, Henry Goerner writing in his book *Thus It Is Written,* related: "God's choice of Abraham had an arbitrary element in it. . . . This selection was not made on the basis of the inherent merit of the man, but on the assumption that he might prove usable for God's purpose. . . . The descendants of Abraham were God's chosen people on the same basis. . . ." Therefore, except as they know and follow God's will, the Jews are no more holy, nor any more favored of God, nor any more excused for their sins, than any other race.

The promises made to Abraham were reconfirmed with Isaac (Genesis 26:2–5), with Jacob (Genesis 28:13–15), and at Sinai with all of Israel. It was there that Moses said: "And because he loved thy fathers, therefore he chose their seed after them, and brought thee out in his sight with his mighty power out of Egypt . . ." (Deuteronomy 4:37).

Israel's national election is unconditional and perpetual; therefore, God will keep His covenant with the nation. Jehovah chose that people and taught the great principles of a holy life to them, and He showed them the way to eternal life. In this world of paganistic, Satan-dominated men, God needed a people He could set apart from the rest of mankind in order to teach His precepts to them.

Therefore, He chose the Jews so that they might learn of Him and then reveal Him to the world, both by precept and example. In *Rebirth of the State of Israel,* Arthur W. Kac suggests: "There is only one sound and logical view by which to account for the indestructibility of the Jews. This view is set forth in the Bible where the survival of the Jews is attributed to the unchangeable will of God, and where the preservation of the Jews is part and parcel of their national destiny as a people chosen of God to fulfill a certain mission in the world."

God's Interest During Dispersion

Webster states that the term *Diaspora* (dispersion) applies collectively to the Jews who were scattered throughout the Old World after the Exile. As you recall, the last group of Jews were taken in the Exile from Israel by Nebuchadnezzar in 586 B.C. A little more than a hundred years earlier, the ten northern tribes had been removed from the Holy Land. For seventy retributive years the Jews were exiled in Babylon, after which some of them returned to Israel. However, many Jews either stayed in Chaldea (Babylon) or dispersed into other areas of the world rather than returning after the Exile.

You will find the promises in God's prophetic Word inspiring concerning Jehovah's interest in the Jews during their centuries of Diaspora. God Himself says ". . . when they are in the land of their enemies, I will not spurn and cast them away, neither will I . . . break My covenant with them" (Leviticus 26:44 AMPLIFIED). Through Jeremiah He declared: ". . . I would no more reject my people than I would change my laws of night and day, of earth and sky. I will never abandon the Jews, or David my servant, or change the plan that his Child will some-day rule these descendants of Abraham, Isaac and Jacob. In-stead I will restore their prosperity and have mercy on them" (Jeremiah 33:25, 26 TLB).

You will note that God is saying that His covenant with Israel is just as binding as the promise of the continuation of day and night. Though the Jews have been wayward, God loves them and will keep His promise made to them. Some Jews have completely forsaken God, even to the point of saying that He does not exist.

On the other hand, many of them ardently follow Jehovah, and the Bible teaches that in the future a revival will break out in Israel, turning many thousands to the Lord. Until that time comes God will be faithful concerning His covenant. Every promise that He ever made to the Jewish people which has not been fulfilled will come to fruition in God's time.

Worldwide Anti-Semitism

Just as Moses foretold, the Israelites were scattered "among all people, from the one end of the earth even unto the other." He also predicted, "And thy life shall hang in doubt before thee; and thou shalt fear day and night, and shalt have none assurance of thy life" (Deuteronomy 28:64,66). None of us doubt the fulfillment of this prophecy many times over. The darkest pages of history have to do with the maltreatment of Jewish people. The nations have seen to it that the Jews have found "no ease," neither have the soles of their feet rested (v. 65). It is true that some countries, especially the United States, have been kinder than others. However, even in this nation we have had our anti-Semitism.

A case in point was the mistreatment of Leon Uris, the famous author of *Exodus*. Writing in a special section of *Strike Zion!* by William Stevenson, Mr. Uris tells of his problems at the hands of his classmates in elementary school in Norfolk, Virginia:

About once every two weeks, for reasons I never learned, I'd find myself looking into a dozen angry faces of kids I played with who were trying to trap me. . . .

At Grammar School 62 in Baltimore a pal of mine had a swastika carved on his cheek with a penknife. It took a lot of them to hold him down. But there were always a lot of them."

There are about fourteen million Jews in the world today. Israel has approximately two and eight-tenths millions (1972), while more than eleven million are scattered throughout the world, with the bulk being in the United States and Russia. The latter has over three million. In early 1972 when President Nixon was making plans to visit Russia later in the spring, a Jewish-American veterans organization asked the President to act as a messiah while in Russia by working for the release of hundreds of thousands of Jews who wanted to leave Russia and enter Israel.

Constant Persecution

History is red with the blood of the Jews. During his reign Antiochus Epiphanes (175–164 B.C.) slaughtered forty thousand Jews and sold that many more into captivity because he said they rejoiced upon hearing a rumor of his death. Then a few years after Christ's death twenty thousand Jews were slain in Caesarea. Later, Damascus went on a rampage and in a single day cut the throats of an estimated ten thousand Jewish people. The trail of blood continued and in A.D. 70 when Jerusalem was destroyed by Titus, one hundred thousand bodies of Jews were thrown over the walls of the city.

During the second century the Romans destroyed about nine

hundred Palestinian towns and villages, killing more than five hundred and fifty thousand men. Not only that, but the so-called holy wars of Europe (1096 and afterward) brought annihilation to countless Jews. Then during the reign of Edward I of England (1272–1307), discriminating laws were enacted. For example, if a Jew struck a Christian, either his right hand was to be cut off, or he was to be killed. The Jew could not appear in public without wearing a certain yellow badge, nor could he enter or leave the country without a license. Some other countries had even more stringent laws.

The Reds and the Nazis Kill

Have you considered that in this century Jews have been banished, tortured, and massacred more than in any other century in history? It is inconceivable that man in this "enlightened" age could be so barbaric. Russia has killed some six million Jews since 1881, and Hitler annihilated a like number in his gas chambers and his other ghastly exterminations. Speaking of Hitler's dastardly acts, a Jewish New York youth was quoted in *Campus Life* magazine recently as saying: "I have to take the annihilation of six million Jews personally. Almost all my relatives were killed there. Everyone else has family reunions. But not at my house."

Some People Hate God

The Scriptures state that the Jews would be hated of all nations, a prediction that doubtless has been fulfilled. Of the fourteen million Jews in the world, many of them outside of Israel are not wanted where they live. Speaking for them, the psalmist says, "Yea, for thy sake are we killed all the day long" (Psalms 44:22).

This passage brings into focus a very serious point; that is, for the sake or cause of God are the Jews killed. This psalm reference is representative of a concept reaching throughout both the Old and the New Testaments; namely, hostility toward the Jews is a disguised hostility toward God Himself. It was Jehovah who instituted the Jewish religious customs, including their holy days. He made the Jews peculiar to other people. God is involved with the Jews, and to oppose them on the grounds named here is to oppose God.

In spite of hatred, persecution, and mass murder, the Jews live on. They could paraphrase Tennyson's poem about the brook and sing, "Nations come and nations go, but we live on forever." Concerning the indestructibility of the Jews, Charles H. Stevens commented in *Prophecy and the Seventies:* "The enigma of history is the preservation of the sons of Jacob. There they stand singularly alone, magnificently different, defiantly unchanged. Like the Bible itself, the descendants of Abraham are standing like a Gibraltar, beat upon by a ceaseless and angry tide of hatred and opposition but still remaining the eternal nation."

Preparation for the Return

In 1897 Theodor Herzi, a Jewish leader, convened the first Zionist Congress in Basle, Switzerland, with the goal, "to create for the Jewish people a home in Palestine secured by public law." But with the Holy Land tightly held by the Turks, the goal appeared totally unattainable. However, the congress was a start.

Then in 1917 the Balfour Declaration was released by England, which stated that Great Britain looked with favor upon "the establishment in Palestine of a national home for the Jewish people." By 1927 there were 150,000 Jews in Palestine. Fulfillment of God's promise that the Jews would be restored had begun. "Thus saith the Lord God; Behold, I will take the children of Israel from among the heathen, whither they be gone, and will gather them on every side, and bring them into their own land. . . . And they shall dwell in the land that I have given unto Jacob my servant, wherein your fathers have dwelt; and they shall dwell therein, even they, and their children, and their children's children for ever" (Ezekiel 37:21,25).

Incidentally, a good way to be sure that references such as this passage in Ezekiel are speaking of a restoration other than that brought about by Nehemiah after the Exile is the use of such statements as "they shall dwell therein, even they, and their children, and their children's children for ever." The restoration after the Exile was not forever.

Prophecy of the Return

The Bible clearly declares that the restoration of the Jews to Palestine would take place after a worldwide dispersion of the people and after a long time of desolation for the Holy Land. Further, the Jews were to return shortly before the Messiah comes to rule. Therefore, it appears evident that at any moment the following three stages, one following the other, could take place: (1) the return of Christ for the Church (the Rapture); (2) the reign of the Antichrist for seven years (the Tribulation); (3) the return of Christ to the earth to end the battle of Armageddon and to set up His one-thousand-year reign (the Millennium).

The prophet Isaiah foretold the return of the Jews: "And in that day the Lord shall again lift up His hand a second time to recover—acquire and deliver—the remnant of His people which is left. . . . And He will raise up a signal for the nations, and will assemble the outcasts of Israel and gather together the dispersed of Judah from the four corners of the earth" (Isaiah 11:11,12 AMPLIFIED).

Note that Isaiah says the Jews would return "the second time." You will remember that the Babylonian Captivity lasted seventy years, after which Nehemiah and his followers returned to Palestine to rebuild the Temple and the city walls. That was the first-time return. Then in A.D. 70 Titus destroyed Jerusalem and the Jews in the Holy Land were dispersed. In his prophecy Isaiah makes it clear that he is talking about a return the "second time." At no time in Jewish history has this prophecy been fulfilled until the last few years.

Of course, the Holy Spirit inspired various prophets to speak of the return. Jeremiah emphasizes the repossession of Palestine (16:5); Isaiah says they will hold the land forever (60:21); and Ezekiel states it will be their own land (36:24). The prophet Amos asserts that the wandering Jew will never have to roam again: "And I bring again the captivity of my people of Israel, and they shall build the waste cities, and inhabit them; and they shall plant vineyards, and drink the wine thereof; they shall also make gardens, and eat the fruit of them. And I will plant them upon their land, and they shall no more be pulled up out of their land which I have given them, saith the Lord thy God" (Amos 9:14,15).

Do Not Misinterpret Scripture

You may have heard someone say that God is through with the Jews. It is said that since they rejected the Messiah, God turned solely and permanently from them to the Gentiles. Any passage, for some reason, which refers to Israel that has not been fulfilled, surely must be referring to the Church, the spiritual Israel. However, such reasoning is ill-founded because it is unscriptural. The fact is, God is not at all through with the Jews, for they figure prominently in predictive Scripture. You will note that Paul referred to the Jews, the Gentiles, and the Church of God (1 Corinthians 10:32), meaning the Jews are, as they have always been, the elect of God; the Gentile is, of course, the non-Jew; while the Church of God is made up of those who are "new creatures in Christ Jesus," whether Jew or Gentile.

The Bible is explicit about the Jews being restored to Palestine the second time (Isaiah 11:11); about their abiding there forever (Joel 3:20); about their never leaving again (Amos 9:15); about God reigning over them through Christ (Micah 4:6,7); and about evil being removed (Zephaniah 3:14,15). Further, you will notice that Jesus Himself referred to a restored Israel during the Tribulation (Matthew 24). Evidently Sabbath laws will be restored (v.20), and the third temple will already be built and sacrifices will be offered (v.15).

The Jews Go Home

A few months ago I flew into the Jan Smuts International Airport in Johannesburg, South Africa. While in that country I learned that Jan Smuts (1870–1950), for whom the airport was named, was for fifteen years prime minister of that country and was a leading twentieth-century statesman. Commenting on the Jews, he once said that the greatest mid-twentieth-century miracle is not the perfection of thermonuclear devices, but the return of the Jews to their ancient homeland precisely as the Bible predicted.

M. R. DeHaan, the well-known radio minister, believed that

the greatest contemporary sign of the coming of Christ is the restoration of the nation of Israel to Palestine. Incidentally, he believed the second most important sign to be the rise of Russia. After World War I the Jews began to return to Palestine in ever-increasing numbers. In his new work on Jewish history entitled *A History of the Jews,* Fredrick Schweitzer says: "Jewish immigration mounted so rapidly after the war that by 1922 Jews accounted for one-ninth, by 1936 one-fifth, by 1945 one-third of the Palestinian population."

On May 14, 1948, Israel declared her independence, which was worked out largely by the Jewish statesmen David Ben-Gurion and Chaim Weizmann. The reestablishment of Israel as a nation after the Jewish people had gone nearly two thousand years without a homeland was a red-letter day in their history.

Planes Fly Them Home

You may know that some Bible scholars feel that the Scriptures speak of the Jews returning by plane. For example, "Who are these that fly as a cloud, and as the doves to their windows" (Isaiah 60:8)? Operation Flying Carpet removed one hundred thousand Jews from Iraq to Israel in 1951 and the previous year fifty thousand were evacuated from Yemen. Many of these people returning from various countries were so thin that a plane could carry two or three times its normal numbers of passengers. Their average weight was a pitiable seventy-eight pounds.

Touching stories are told of those airlifts. There was the emaciated old man borne on the back of his skinny son. Upon deplaning he slipped from his son's back, and upon his hands and knees he kissed the ground of his beloved promised land. Then he died.

Arriving mostly by plane, the Jews have come from around the world to live in the sovereign state of Israel. The Bible says, "Ye have seen what I did unto the Egyptians, and how I bare you on eagles' wings, and brought you unto myself" (Exodus 19:4). Eagles' wings became more than just a manner of speaking, for the giant metal "eagles" have ferried the Jews to Israel by the hundreds of thousands.

Israel Today

If you have been to Israel within the last few years you found a little country buzzing with activity. Already the desert is blossoming "as a rose" (Isaiah 35:1) and barren hillsides and mosquito-infested lowlands are giving way to bountiful yields season after season. Israel is one of only six countries in the world that has a surplus food supply. This fact is incredible when you remember that as late as 1948 the consensus of world opinion was that a people could hardly even survive there! This, too, is fulfillment of Scripture: "The land now desolate shall be tilled, instead of lying waste for every passer-by to see. Men will say that this same land which was waste has become like a garden of Eden . . ." (Ezekiel 36:34,35 NEB).

Israel has now been restored to Palestine in fulfillment of many promises in the Bible. As you can imagine, many orthodox Jews realize that they have returned under the guidance of God, and now they are intently asking Him to send the Messiah, not realizing that Jesus Christ is that promised Redeemer. The Reverend James E. Marks, a Jew converted to Christianity, writing in *The Church of God Evangel,* tells of a recent visit to the famed Wailing Wall located in the old temple area in Jerusalem: "Men were swaying back and forth with perspiration pouring from their faces; they were lost in worship to God.

They were saying, 'I believe with perfect faith in the coming of the Messiah: and though he tarry, I will wait faithfully for his coming' [a daily prayer of the Jews]."

God Is With Israel

Though Israel as a nation has not yet returned to God, God has His hand on that people. He is behind the massive, world-wide move of the Jews returning to Palestine. Further, it was no happenstance that the Dead Sea scrolls were found only a few months before Israel became a nation.

In March, 1970, at Qumran I stood with a friend on the ruins of a Jewish settlement that dated back to about 100 B.C. Pointing to the side of a cliff, my friend identified the entrance to the cave where the scrolls were found. With the Dead Sea and a brisk wind at my back, I gazed westward across the narrow ravine at that cave opening and wondered at the marvelous care of the Almighty. He had kept those scrolls hidden and intact for more than two thousand years! Then just before Israel became a nation the scrolls were found, and at the first meeting of the Israeli Parliament on May 15, 1948, a photostatic copy of the fortieth chapter of Isaiah from the newly-discovered Dead Sea scrolls was at the desk of every member of that body. That chapter, directed to Israel and yet to be fulfilled, begins as follows: "Comfort, oh, comfort my people, says your God. Speak tenderly to Jerusalem and tell her that her sad days are gone. Her sins are pardoned, and the Lord will give her twice as many blessings as he gave her punishment before" (Isaiah 40:1,2 TLB). What a beautiful promise to a people who have been hounded, tortured and killed for centuries. Within the first half of this century alone nearly twelve million Jewish people were murdered, but now God's promise given through Isaiah is in sight. His people are back in their land, and ere long their Messiah will return and pardon their sins.

Jacob's Day of Trouble

In your study of the Scriptures you have noted that the Bible teaches that the Jews would return to Israel, Christ would translate the Church, and then the Jews would undergo the Tribulation while in their homeland. In fact, the passages referring to that seven-year period are directed chiefly to God's elect, the Jews. Christ talks exclusively to the Israelites in the Olivet Discourse (Matthew 24). However, the Bible also reveals that the Tribulation will be upon all nations of the earth, and will affect both Jew and Gentile. Jeremiah describes those days of Tribulation: "Alas! for that day is great, so that none is like it. It is the time of Jacob's trouble; but he shall be saved out of it" (30:7 BERKELEY).

When the Rapture takes the believers from the earth, that event will probably cause many Jews to rethink their stand concerning Jesus Christ, and some will turn to Him. As was stated earlier, the 144,000 Jewish evangelists will convert untold numbers of both Jews and Gentiles during the seven-year Tribulation.

A New Heart For Israel

You will notice that the Bible foretells a spiritual regeneration of the returning people. This is significant in light of the low spiritual condition of many Jews today. Though some of them may be cold, calculating and godless, Ezekiel promises: "A new heart also will I give you, and a new spirit will I put within you: and I will take away the stony heart out of your flesh, and I will give you an heart of flesh. And I will put my spirit within you, and cause you to walk in my statutes, and ye shall keep my judgments, and do them. And ye shall dwell in the land that I gave to your fathers; and ye shall be my people, and I will be your God" (Ezekiel 36:26–28).

You will find in the Scriptures that time and again Israel's return to the land of the Book is connected with a return to the God of the Book. Jehovah promises to "change the speech of my returning people to pure Hebrew so that all can worship the Lord together" (Zephaniah 3:9 TLB). Israel is now ripe for revival, for already, pure Hebrew is the official speech throughout the land.

Christ, King of the Jews

God will keep His covenant with Israel to bring revival, not because she is worthy, but because He loves His people, and because His Word has declared it. Instead of people slaying the Jew, they will turn to him: ". . . it shall come to pass, that ten men shall take hold out of all languages of the nations, even shall take hold of the skirt of him that is a Jew, saying, We will go with you: for we have heard that God is with you" (Zechariah 8:23).

The Jews have not been permanently turned aside. The inscription on the cross which read, "This is Jesus the King of the Jews" (Matthew 27:37) was prophetic. He is King, and someday Israel will accept Him. ". . . they will look on him they pierced, and mourn for him as for an only son . . ." (Zephaniah 12:10 TLB).

Presently, Israel is dubious of Christ, saying that He was not the true Messiah. Therefore, they do not accept Christianity. At a press conference in Chicago not long ago, Billy Graham told of his first visit to the Holy Land some years ago. At that time Golda Meir, now premier, was secretary of state.

"Have you come to proselyte the Jews for Christianity," she queried. "No," answered Graham, "I have come to Israel for two reasons. First, to visit your country which I have long wanted to do. Second, because I want to understand clearly what you believe about God and share with you and your people what I believe about Him. You see, I have already been proselyted by a Jew myself, Jesus." This conversation was the beginning of a fast friendship between the evangelist and Mrs. Meir.

The Third Temple

In order to take a look at another important happening at Jerusalem, we must go back to the beginning of the Tribulation when the temple will be built. Of course, it could be constructed before the Lord raptures the Church. On the other hand, you can well understand how its construction could quickly be done just afterward. But build the third temple the Jews will, for they have every intention of doing so, and God's Word predicts it (Acts 15:16, and other references).

As far back as 1967 the *Washington Post* newspaper carried a large ad calling for help to build the third temple. "Executive talent, adminstrators, and workers on all levels are needed," it stated. Shortly after the Six-Day War, *Time* magazine gave almost a page to an article speculating on the third temple. Rumor has it that the temple has already been prefabricated and can be put up at a moment's notice, while another rumor declares that though it is not prefabricated, detailed plans have been drawn.

Be that as it may, we cannot be certain when or even where in Jerusalem the temple will be built. It is generally thought that it will be constructed on the ancient site of Solomon's Temple. As you know, Christ Himself spoke of the holy place, a part of the temple, in the Olivet Discourse (Matthew 24:15). Also, Paul made reference to the temple when speaking of the Antichrist who "sitteth in the temple of God" (2 Thessalonians 2:4).

Next Year In Jerusalem

For centuries the Jewish toast at the annual Passover was "Next year in Jerusalem," meaning that the next year the Jews hoped to be back in the homeland. Now many of them are back. Their country is prospering and it has world significance. Someday Christ Himself will return to Jerusalem, arriving on the Mount of Olives (Zechariah 14:4), and from that city He will rule the earth in a thousand years of peace.

We do not know when He will set up His reign, but it could be within the next few years. *Shalom,* the common greeting used throughout Israel today, will truly mean peace then, for the Lord Jesus, who is the Prince of Peace, will lead the world during a millennium of tranquility.

7

Doomsday

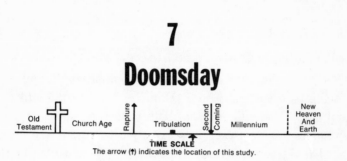

TIME SCALE
The arrow (↑) indicates the location of this study.

The world is headed for upheaval and destruction of catastrophic proportions. A time is coming when half of the earth's population will die within a few years time. If this sounds like the talk of a prophet of doom, it is meant to, for that is exactly what awaits the world—doom. It is understandable that Jesus, when referring to those horrendous days, called them a time of "Great Tribulation." He said that unless those times were shortened, all mankind would perish.

You will find that more of the Scriptures are given to the seven-year Tribulation than to any other corresponding length of time in history, with the probable exception of Christ's last years on earth. The prophet Jeremiah called it "the time of Jacob's trouble" (30:7); Ezekiel named the period a "furnace" for melting Israel (22:19–22); Daniel, "a time of trouble" (12:1); Joel referred to those days as "a day of darkness and of gloominess" (2:2); while Jesus admonished people to pray that they might be able to escape that period (Luke 21:36). In the Book of Revelation, John devotes fourteen chapters (6–19) to the subject. Jesus said, ". . . those will be days of such horror as

have never been since the beginning of God's creation. . ."
(Mark 13:19 TLB).

The Other Half

Earlier we looked at the first half of the Tribulation and now
we will study the latter half. The Bible identifies the Tribulation
as being a seven-year period (Daniel 9:27), divided into two
equal parts. You will find that both testaments speak of these
two halves, dividing each into exactly three and a half years.
Daniel divided the period by pointing out incidents "in the
midst of the week" (9:27; see also Daniel 12:7), while the
Apocalypse refers to "a time, and times, and half a time" (Revelation 12:14).

The Bible declares that the length of each period will be
forty-two months (Revelation 11:2; 13:5), and other references
even give the number of the days as being 1,260 (Revelation
11:3; 12:6). You will note that even though the Tribulation is
divided into two parts, the parts are closely integrated, making
up a whole (Daniel 9:27). Hence, they are not two periods
separated by a span of time, but the latter immediately follows
the former.

A Look Backward

You will remember our looking at some predicted events that
evidently will happen during the first half of the Tribulation. It
is believed that in the beginning the Antichrist will secure his
position by pulling world powers to himself. Understandably,
he will try to crush those who refuse to cooperate. The reason
Russia and her allies invade Palestine may be not only to destroy that little country and take spoils, but also to get at the

Antichrist and his forces who will be allies of Israel. Of course, the Reds will be providentially stopped.

Also, during the first three and a half years the apostate church will be a close ally of the Antichrist and it will have great influence over him (Revelation 17:3). Further, the Two Witnesses (Revelation 11) will minister and will turn thousands to God; they will call down fire, cause droughts, strike people dead, and be a general hindrance to Antichrist.

As you read the scriptural account of the events leading up to the end of the first half of the Tribulation, you will see that apparently things will begin to happen in quick succession. Russia will fall (Ezekiel 39:4–6), the apostate church will be crushed (Revelation 17:16), and the Two Witnesses will be killed. When these things happen, though not necessarily in the order listed here, then the Antichrist will usher in the last three and a half years of the Tribulation by committing "the abomination of desolation" (Daniel 9:27).

What Is the Abomination of Desolation?

Jesus, quoting Daniel, referred to a grave breach of Jewish worship which will take place in the middle of the Tribulation. He said, " 'So when you see "the abomination of desolation", of which the prophet Daniel spoke, standing in the holy place (let the reader understand), then those who are in Judaea must take to the hills' " (Matthew 24:15,16 NEB).

Satan, who instigates the activities of the Antichrist (Revelation 13:2), has always wanted to be worshiped. He even tried to get Christ to worship him during the wilderness temptation. Therefore, with the apostate church out of the way and the Two Witnesses murdered, he will have a free hand in religious matters. This is when he will break his agreement with Israel and will blatantly demand that Israel and the rest of the world worship him on penalty of death (Revelation 13:12,15). The Apostle Paul speaks of that event: "Let no one in any way deceive you; for the apostasy is to come first, and the man of sin is to be revealed, the son of doom, the adversary, so proudly insolent toward everything called God or worshiped as to seat himself in the temple of God with the acclaim that he himself is God" (2 Thessalonians 2:3,4 BERKELEY).

You will note that Paul says the Antichrist will seat himself in the Jewish temple, the place of worship which the Israelis highly revere. But there this godless man will be, brashly proclaiming that he is God. This gross sacrilege will fulfill the abomination of desolation prediction which is a desecration of the temple by a Gentile entering the holy place. As you may know, the holy place was a section of the temple that only an authorized priest was allowed to enter. Such an abomination occurred another time when in 165 B.C. a conqueror by the name of Antiochus Epiphanes actually slaughtered a swine in the holy place.

Flee For Your Lives!

If you will read such references as Revelation 3:10, 7:9–14, and Isaiah 34:2, you will find it evident that the Tribulation will be worldwide in scope. Though this is a fact, that seven-year period is spoken of in the Bible especially in relation to Israel (see Daniel 9:24 and Matthew 24). God told Daniel that the time was reckoned upon *thy* people, and upon *thy* holy city. Therefore the Jews are in focus at the time of the Tribulation, though the whole world is included also. Jesus, addressing the Jews, said that when they see the Antichrist desecrate the temple, "let them which be in Judea flee into the mountains" (Matthew 24:16).

Of course, the reason for fleeing will be to escape the wrath of the Satan-directed Antichrist. It is worth mentioning here that the ancient area of Petra is located in the hills about fifty miles south of the Dead Sea. Enclosed by sandstone cliffs brightly veined with varied shades of red, purple and yellow, this site of earlier civilizations, dating back thousands of years, is approached from the east through a narrow gorge nearly a mile and a half long. Though at times people resided there, it was occupied for hundreds of years only by wandering tribesmen. Many Bible scholars believe this to be the area that God has preserved for those Jews who will escape the Antichrist. Petra is located in Biblical Moab, and the Scriptures state that the land of Moab "shall escape out of his [Antichrist's] hand" (Daniel 11:41). The Lord will assist the Jewish people with their escape into the wilderness (Revelation 12:6,13,14), and when Antichrist sets out to destroy them, a great earthquake will wipe out his forces (Revelation 12:16).

Antichrist Blasphemes God

Bent on being worshiped, the Antichrist curses God, the house of worship, and the raptured saints. Revelation states: "And he opened his mouth in blasphemy against God, to blaspheme his name, and his tabernacle, and them that dwell in heaven" (13:6). This Anti-God world leader will do all within his power to tear down every vestige of worship of the Trinity. Clyde C. Cox comments in his *Apocalyptic Commentary:* "The beast is an atheist . . . To promulgate his atheist claim, he will be antagonistic toward any mode of worship or place of worship, even the tabernacles or church houses. The name of our

God or of our Lord Jesus Christ will become the target of his persecution; he will curse the name of God." Daniel says that he "shall speak marvelous things against the God of gods" (11:36).

Robbing Israel of the choice to worship God (Daniel 9:-27), he instead will demand that Israel and the whole earth actually worship him. As was mentioned earlier, you should note how often the word *worship* is used in Revelation 13 in reference to the Antichrist. More than likely, the badge of allegiance to worship will be "the mark of the beast" (Revelation 13:16,17). If one does not take the mark, he cannot buy or sell. Hence, the ultimatum will be, "Worship me or starve!"

When Heaven Is Quiet

God will rain judgment upon the earth during the Tribulation, and this trial of mankind will refine a portion of Jewry which will accept Christ as King when He returns from the saints (Zechariah 12:10); it will also prove many Gentiles who will receive Christ and go into the millennial kingdom. Mostly, however, the judgments of God will prove the wantonness of practically all of the world which, though under severe trial, will curse God, openly defying Him (Revelation 16:9).

Earlier, we studied some of the seal judgments described in Revelation. Now, as the seventh seal is opened (8:1), a silence of thirty minutes covers heaven as all of God's celestial beings anticipate the awesome times to follow upon earth. The seventh seal judgment in turn introduces the trumpet judgments (8:7 – 9:21; 11:15–19), the last three of which are apparently even harsher than the others. They are referred to as woes.

John's Four Trumpets

The first trumpet (Revelation 8:7). Evangelical commentators take this reference literally. It states that a third of earth, trees, and grass will be ruined by hail and fire raining down mingled with blood. This terrible judgment is reminiscent of the Egyptian plagues of the Old Testament. This will be a horrible time, but it is only the introduction of worse devastation to follow.

The second trumpet (vs. 8,9). This judgment destroys a third of the world's shipping, and a third of the sea turns to blood, killing a third of sea life. What an awful time when God's mercy turns to wrath!

The third trumpet (vs. 10,11). With this judgment a third of the fresh water of the world is polluted by some sort of mass from outer space entering the atmosphere, understandably burning, and probably causing a fallout problem that somehow affects drinking water. So severe is this problem of poisoning that "many men died of the waters."

The fourth trumpet (vs. 12,13). Whereas the first three trumpets had to do with the earth and sea, this judgment has to do with the heavens. In speaking of the Tribulation, Jesus foretold "signs in the sun, and in the moon, and in the stars . . ." (Luke 21:25). Now, here in Revelation, John declares that a third of the sun, moon, and stars will be darkened. Someone made the observation that progressively, devastation is brought upon the earth in the following order: (1) food is destroyed; (2) shipping is hampered; (3) usable water is limited; and (4) production is hindered. In his work *The Revelation of Jesus Christ,* John F. Walvoord observed: "The four trumpets deal with aspects of the physical world which are taken more or less for granted. . . . So dramatic are the judgments and so unmistakably an evidence of the power and sovereignty of God that blaspheming men on earth can no longer ignore the fact that God is dealing with them."

When People Cannot Die

John's fifth trumpet, which is also called the first woe, is more severe than the foregoing trumpet judgments. You will note in Revelation 9 that this first woe has to do with hordes of demons in the likeness of stinging scorpions released from hell to sting people for five months. You should read the sober account of these hideous creatures:

> And it was commanded them that they should not hurt the grass of the earth, neither any green thing, neither any tree; but only those men which have not the seal of God in their foreheads. And to them it was given that they should not kill them, but that they should be tormented five months: and their torment was as the torment of a scorpion, when he striketh a man. And in those days shall men seek death, and shall not find it; and shall desire to die, and death shall flee from them. (Revelation 9:4–6)

John continues to discuss these spirit beings through the eleventh verse, carefully describing their fierce physical appearance.

These scorpions will sting everybody except the redeemed Jews and, surely, those Gentiles who have believed in Christ. Their sting is almost unbearable, the pain being so frightening that people would rather die. Their not being able to do so for five months probably refers to their being under the power of the demons, thus being unable to exercise their own will in committing suicide.

Hundreds of years before Patmos, Joel foretold the coming of these same creatures (2:1–10), saying that ". . . they shall climb up upon the houses; they shall enter in at the windows like a thief" (v. 9).

Such a hellish creature as this is difficult for us to imagine, but we have no reason to give this scriptural account anything but a literal interpretation. Though some people today do not believe that the devil exists, men then will believe these demon-beings are real when they are painfully stung for five months. You can imagine that brilliant scientists will quickly prepare a sure-kill pesticide, but these little beings will buzz through and beyond the preparation, because men cannot kill a demon.

When Half Of Mankind Dies

The term *woe* in the Scriptures refers to some great calamity which is usually a judgment from God. The second woe, which is the sixth trumpet judgment described by John, is introduced by reminding us that "One woe is past; and behold, there come two woes more hereafter" (Revelation 9:12). Revelation 9:-13–15 infers that this devastating second woe comes about partially as an answer to the prayers of persecuted followers of God. The incident has to do with four angels being released at a set time whose task it is to slay one-third of mankind. These four angels may be evil spirits whom God permits to be loosened. The judgment is one of the most far-reaching that takes place during the Tribulation. The death of these millions plus those killed earlier in the fourth seal (6:7,8) adds up to the death of half the world's populace within a short time.

Commenting on this second woe, Hal Lindsey stated in his book *The Late Great Planet Earth:* "Immediately after their release an incredible army emerges from the Euphrates . . . it numbers 200 million (Revelation 9:16). . . . They will wipe out a third of the earth's population (Revelation 9:18) . . . by fire, smoke (or air pollution), and brimstone (or melted earth) . . . many Bible expositors believe that this is an accurate first-century description of a twentieth-century thermonuclear war."

The Vials of Wrath

The third woe which John announces has to do with the very end of the age. Known also as the seventh trumpet of judgment (Revelation 11:14–19), this time has to do, in part, with voices from heaven announcing in unison: "The kingdoms of this world are become the kingdoms of our Lord, and of his Christ; and he shall reign for ever and ever" (v. 15). However, before Christ returns and sets up His reign, Revelation's seven bowl or vial judgments must take place. These incredibly horrible times may come within the last few months or even the last weeks of the Tribulation.

Those will be days of inconceivable hardship. For thousands of years our loving Father has withheld judgment that wicked men deserved. Now He will deter no longer, for mankind will have fully demonstrated that it has absolutely no intention of honoring or obeying God (9:20,21).

The first vial (16:2) brings "horrible, malignant sores . . . on everyone who had the mark . . ." (TLB). Only those who have not taken the mark of the beast will escape this plague.

The second vial (v. 3) turns the seas to blood, killing every living thing in them, and doubtlessly sending up an unbearable stench on seacoasts around the world. Whereas the second trumpet judgment turned one-third of the sea to blood, this second vial judgment appears to affect all seas. You will remember that 72 percent of the earth's surface is water, and you can well understand the devastating effect of this plague.

The third vial (vs. 4–7) turns the fresh water of the world into blood. Just as evil men have shed the blood of countless "saints and prophets," God now gives "them blood to drink; for they are worthy . . ." (v. 6). In this reference the angel justifies God's judgments, saying, "Even so, Lord God Almighty, true and righteous are thy judgments" (v. 7). Thousands upon thousands of God's followers will be killed during the Tribulation, and this plague will be in retribution for that bloodletting.

The fourth vial (vs. 8,9) intensifies the heat of the sun so that men will be "scorched with great heat" (v. 9), yet John says they ". . . blasphemed the name of God . . . and they repented not to give him glory." You may know people who believe that wicked men would repent if they were brought under the direct judgment of God, and perhaps some of them would, but these accounts of the last days demonstrate that wicked men will curse God at the end-time during judgment.

The fifth vial (vs. 10,11) deals with the very capital of the world ruler along with the entire world. Like some of the plagues of Egypt, this judgment brings darkness, sores and intense pain. The Bible says "they gnawed their tongues for pain" (v. 10), and blasphemed God because of their extreme suffering.

The sixth vial (vs. 12–16) dries up the Euphrates river, which had recently been turned to blood. Isaiah (11:15) and Zechariah (10:11) also predict the drying up of the Euphrates, though they do not name the river. This permits passage across the riverbed "of the kings of the east" (Revelation 16:12) as they go to

Palestine to fight in the battle of Armageddon (v. 14). These kings are apparently oriental, coming from countries such as Red China and others.

The seventh vial (vs. 17-21) is accompanied by the announcement, "It is done," (v. 17) meaning that the end has come. The destruction that then breaks loose is incredible. Note what happens: (1)"voices, and thunders, and lightnings;" (2)"a great earthquake" the like of which has never been before, apparently making shambles of all world capitals. Besides, every island sinks, and mountains crumble; (3)hailstones weighing a hundred pounds batter the earth. Little wonder that Jesus said if those days were not shortened, nobody could survive!

Are you tempted to say that these hideous things could never happen, that these Scriptural references are some sort of symbolism and are not to be taken literally? If so, remember that God has done some of these very things before when He sent the ten plagues upon Egypt more than three thousand years ago (Exodus 7-12). At that time He turned water to blood, caused sores, hail, locusts, and darkness. God has lost none of His power. Therefore, at the end of this age He will again carry out plagues such as fell on Egypt, except this time they will be more severe and will affect the whole earth.

The Battle of Armageddon

While the judgments of God are being poured out upon the world, man's inhumanity to man will add additional misery. For example, it may well be that such atrocities as were committed at Hitler's Buchenwald and Dachau will be repeated many times over, carried out by Antichrist and his godless forces. Also, it seems that war will rage during a good deal of the last half of the Tribulation.

It has been commonly believed that Armageddon will be a single battle lasting only a few days, but that does not seem to be what the Bible actually says. It states that spirits of hell will gather the kings of the earth "to the battle of that great day of God Almighty" (Revelation 16:14). The account continues: "And he gathered them together into a place called in the Hebrew tongue Armageddon" (v. 16).

In his book entitled *Things To Come,* J. Dwight Pentecost reckons: "The extent of this great movement in which God deals with the kings of the earth and of the whole world (Revelation 16:14) will not be seen unless it is realized that the battle of that great day of God Almighty (Revelation 16:14) is not an isolated battle, but rather a campaign that extends over the last half of the Tribulation period. The Greek word *polemos,* translated "battle" in Revelation 16:14, signifies a war or campaign . . . . " Many Bible scholars think that the battle (campaign) of Armageddon will last throughout the last three and a half years of the Tribulation.

Time of Armageddon

At the surrender of Japan which ended World War II, General Douglas MacArthur said: "If we do not devise some greater and more equitable system, Armageddon will be at our door." He knew the holocaust of war, and he feared it. Yet, as you know, we have not found that more equitable system, and there is a constant fear of a global conflict. In 1967 former President Eisenhower said that unless peace can be negotiated, then Armageddon will soon follow, and President Kennedy stated, "mankind must put an end to war, or war will put an end to mankind." This final, global war that politicians fear is graphically described in the Bible.

As has been pointed out, Armageddon will be a campaign, not a single battle, and the nations will be called together by Satan to fight it. Though the nations come at the instigation of Satan, God will deal with the armies of the world because of their mistreatment of Israel (Joel 3:2), because of their great wrongdoings (Revelation 19:15), and because of their utter godlessness (16:9).

The Place of Armageddon

The Bible says that the armies of the world will be summoned to a place "called in the Hebrew tongue Armageddon" (Revelation 16:16). Armageddon is sometimes rendered *Har-Megiddo, har* meaning mountain, and *megiddo* meaning slaughter. Megiddo is in the Holy Land. Can you imagine all the armies of the earth converging on Palestine? Years ago the prophet Joel wrote of that day: "Proclaim ye this among the Gentiles; Prepare war, wake up the mighty men, let all the men of war draw near; let them come up: Beat your plowshares into swords, and your pruninghooks into spears; let the weak say, I am strong. Assemble yourselves. . . . Let the heathen be wakened, and come up to the valley of Jehoshaphat" (3:9-12). God speaking through Zechariah said, "I will gather all nations against Jerusalem to battle . . . " (14:2). In his book *Expository Sermons on Revelation,* volume 5, W. A. Criswell commented: "These armies will be converging on Palestine. Enemies will gather from every side. It will be a war to exterminate Israel; it will be a war of nation against nation; and it will be a war against God."

Plain of Megiddo

As I rode across the plain of Megiddo, the site of Armageddon, a few months ago, I tried to imagine the magnitude of the coming final campaign of the ages to take place there. While musing on the conflagration, I remembered that the plain is fourteen by twenty miles in size, and is one of the most natural battlefields in all the world. Thousands of years ago Thothmes III of Egypt said, "Megiddo is worth a thousand cities," while Napoleon allegedly remarked that it was the most ideal location on earth for a battle.

Campaign of Armageddon

You will note from the Scriptures that the great military campaign of the end-times will include several battles and will probably take place over an extended period of time. Besides Megiddo, there is to be a battle in the valley of Jehosaphat (Joel 3:2,13), which seems to be an area east of Jerusalem. Also, in two different chapters Isaiah speaks of the Lord coming from Edom or Idumea, which is south of Jerusalem (see Isaiah 34; 63). Further, Jerusalem is graphically described as the site of conflict (Zechariah 12:2-11; 14:2). Therefore, it seems evident that the campaign will extend from Megiddo on the north to Edom on the south, thus covering about all of Palestine.

It would appear that during the latter half of the Tribulation Antichrist will have his headquarters in Palestine (Daniel 11:-45) and the armies of the East will invade and attack his forces (Revelation 16:12-16). The Western powers which will be the extended old Roman empire, and quite probably including the United States, will be on the side of Antichrist. The nations of the South will be involved also. Russia will have been destroyed earlier (Ezekiel 38,39). Some Bible students believe that Russia's invasion of Palestine and her subsequent destruction at the middle of the Tribulation will trigger the Armageddon campaign which will last throughout the last three and a half years of the Tribulation.

A Summary of Armageddon

When you take a look at what the Bible says about the end-time, you find it frightening indeed. With mass media coverage of world events, you can well imagine television sets around the world giving out the awesome news in ghastly detail as one event after the other takes place, including the judgments of God as well as the battles of Armageddon.

In summing up the military conflicts of that day, the following seems to be the order: (1)The armies of the southern confederacy are defeated (mentioned in Daniel 11:40); (2)Russia and her allies invade Israel and are destroyed by God (Ezekiel 38; 39); (3)Antichrist breaks his pact with Israel and then occupies the Holy Land (Daniel 11:41-45); thus, with the northern confederacy and the confederacy of the southern nations out of the way, the massive armies of the East are the only threat to Antichrist and his forces; (4)Then these Asiatic powers invade Palestine (Revelation 16:14) in preparation for the climactic battle of the Tribulation.

Signs in the Sky

In your study of the Olivet Discourse, have you noticed Christ's comment about the very last days of the Tribulation? He said: "And then shall appear the sign of the Son of Man in heaven . . . " (Matthew 24:30), inferring that some phenomenon will occur in the sky just before He returns. We do not know what the sign will be, but the Scriptures do reveal man's reaction to it. The armies of the East and those of Antichrist will forget their differences and will give their sole attention to the heavens, apparently trying to blast Christ out of the sky. John declares: "And I saw the beast, and the kings of the earth, and their armies, gathered together to make war against him that sat on the horse, and against his army" (Revelation 19:19; see also Zechariah 14:3; Revelation 17:14; 19:11-21).

The Second Coming of Christ

While the armies of the earth are poised to make war against Christ, He will suddenly burst upon the scene and literally destroy those armies "with the brightness of his coming" (2 Thessalonians 2:8). Evidently, our Lord will employ atomic fission at this time, the secret of which He knew a long time before Einstein ever dreamed of splitting the atom.

You will notice that the Bible describes that terrible day when hordes of Christ's enemies will actually melt away from Him. Zechariah graphically portrays the scene: "Their flesh shall consume away while they stand upon their feet, and their eyes shall consume away in their holes, and their tongue shall consume away in their mouth" (14:12). The remnant will meet death when they are slain by Christ, and the fowls will eat their flesh (Revelation 19:21).

Christ the King will first touch the earth on the Mount of Olives, the very hill from which He ascended. At that time Olivet will divide, forming a great valley (Zechariah 14:3,4,8; Ezekiel 47:8-10).

Our Redeemer will return from heaven as King of kings and Lord of lords (Revelation 19:16), and all of His glorified believers will accompany Him (Jude 14,15). In quick succession He will destroy the Antichrist and his lieutenant (Revelation 19:-

20), and He will have Satan bound and cast into hell where he will remain for a thousand years (Revelation 20:1-3). Since no unsaved person can enter the millennial age (Zechariah 13:9; Matthew 25:30,46), Christ will judge those living upon the earth when the Tribulation ends. The righteous will be admitted into the Milennium, and the wicked will suffer eternal punishment.

Christ, who is the Prince of Peace, will then rule this entire world for a thousand years. Purity of motive, holiness in worship, and universal peace will be as common then as sin, apostasy and war are today. May God speed that day!

8
After Sunrise

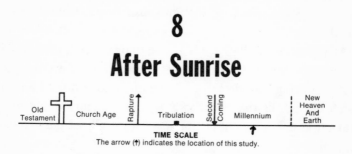

TIME SCALE
The arrow (✝) indicates the location of this study.

The thousand-year reign of Christ upon earth will break forth like a beautiful, cloudless day after a night of violent storm. Just as the Tribulation will be a period of upheavel, disorder and destruction, the thousand years following it will be, in contrast, a time of tranquility, order, and peace. That age will be known as the Millennium. The word *millennium* comes from two Latin words meaning a thousand years, and six times in Revelation 20:1-7 the Bible refers to that blessed and benevolent time lasting a thousand years.

The Lord Jesus Himself will be the world Ruler then, and peace will spread around the globe. For a thousand years there will be almost no sickness, hence no clinics, hospitals, or asylums. Doctors will have to turn to other professions, and pharmaceutical firms will be nonexistent. Funeral parlors will not be common, because sickness and death will be at a minimum. Also, there will be no more war.

Can you imagine a time when there will be no talk of war? These days the news media constantly report that some nation is fighting another somewhere, but then war will not exist, nor will the awful pain and sorrow which accompany it. Also, violence in the streets and homes will be unknown. Apparently during the Millennium there will be no jails, no prisons, and no places of teen-age detention. Righteousness will reign throughout the earth.

As you know, millions now starve to death each year, and it is said that half of the world goes to bed hungry every night. Not so during the blessed Millennium. The Word of God is careful to tell us that everybody will have plenty to eat then. Hunger and famine will be unknown when Christ the Messiah rules the world.

Jesus Will Return to Earth

You were probably appalled earlier as we studied the scriptural account of the Tribulation. The stern judgments of God coupled with the awesome demon-motivated crimes of the Antichrist will make for a time of indescribable pain and sorrow for mankind. However, when it looks as though man will be completely annihilated, Christ will return from Heaven accompanied by the saints, including you and me, if we will have gone earlier with Him in the Rapture. In quick succession He will end the war of Armageddon, cast Antichrist and the False Prophet into hell, judge all living men, have Satan bound and cast into the bottomless pit, and then set up His millennial reign here upon earth.

Do you find it difficult to comprehend that Christ will be the world Ruler right here in this old world? Since His theocratic government will be so utterly different from any system in the world today, comprehension of it does not come easy. Nonetheless He will rule the world from Jerusalem, the same city where He was once crucified. His great society programs will truly be great, and His holy plans for world peace will really work. What a magnificent day it will be when Jesus rules the earth!

Jesus Judges Living Men

You will find in your Bible study that everybody will not be destroyed at Armageddon. Of course, many people will not be involved in that war and will live on after its conclusion. It is these people that Christ talks about being judged (Matthew 25:31-46) "When the Son of man shall come in his glory . . . . " Concerning that time, the psalmist declared: " . . . for he cometh to judge the earth: he shall judge the world with righteousness, and the people with his truth" (96:13); and Luke wrote: "Because he hath appointed a day in the which he will judge the world in righteousness by that man whom he hath ordained . . . " (Acts 17:31).

There seem to be several judgments that will take place just before the beginning of the Millennium. Not only will the Antichrist and the False Prophet be judged and cast into hell (Revelation 19:20), and Satan bound and cast into the bottomless pit, but both the living Jews and the Gentiles will be judged.

The Jews Are Judged

Designed to keep rebels out of the Millennium, this judgment will have to do with all Jews alive at that time. Described by the prophet Ezekiel, that judgment will deal with all Jews who survived the Tribulation (Ezekiel 20:37,38). Jesus referred to that judgment in a parable (Matthew 25:14-30).

In Matthew 24:30,31 Jesus said that the angels " . . . shall gather together his elect [the Jews] from the four winds." Matthew 25:30 says that the "unprofitable servant" will be cast out, but the good and faithful servant will be told to "enter thou into the joy of thy lord" (v. 23). Those that are found to belong to God will enter the Millennium in their earthly bodies.

Only the converted will enter the Millennium. Daniel says, "But the saints of the most High shall take the kingdom, and possess the kingdom for ever, even for ever and ever" (7:18), and he repeats himself in verse 22 and also in verse 27. He seems to be emphasizing that no blashphemer, no rejector, no sinner will have any place in the glorious, righteous kingdom. Such persons will be denied admittance to both the kingdom and eternal life (see Ezekiel 20:37 and Matthew 25:30).

The Gentiles Are Judged, Too

Out of the more than three and one-half billion people in the world today, only about fourteen million are Jews. If that ratio still exists at the end of the Tribulation, you can readily see that most of the people living will be non-Jews, or Gentiles. Nonetheless, since Jews are the race God chose to work through thousands of years ago in order in win the world, much of the Scriptures differentiates between the Jew and the Gentile right up to and, in fact, through the Millennium.

You will notice that the Bible speaks of the judgment of the Gentiles who survive the Tribulation. Taking place "When the Son of man shall come in his glory . . . " (Matthew 25:31-46), this judgment will be upon individuals rather than nations. Bible students believe that *Gentiles* is a better translation than *heathen* or *nations*. The individual non-Jews will be judged on the basis of their regeneration, just as the Jews will be.

Treatment of the Brethren

It seems that the criterion for acceptance at this judgment will rest upon treatment of "my brethren" (Matthew 25:40), apparently speaking of the Jews of the Tribulations. The lines will be so emphatically drawn during the Tribulation that apparently the only reason a Gentile will befriend the persecuted Jew will be due to the Gentile's love and acceptance of God. In other words, it appears that only born-again people will help the born-again Jew during the last half of the Tribulation. If the Gentile feeds, clothes, or visits the Jew (see Matthew 25:35,36), he will do so at the risk of his very life, and he will not do that unless the love of God dwells in his heart.

The Gentiles who are thus found to possess the new birth will be admitted to the kingdom (Matthew 25:34). Those who opposed God's people will be denied entrance (v. 41). Just how this judgment will be carried out on Gentiles throughout the world, we are not told. We do know that a great judgment will take place in the valley of Jehoshaphat (Joel 3:2). Surely God's records will show each individual's inner thoughts and intent toward the persecuted Jew, wherever in the world the Gentile lives.

Your Place in That Judgment

The Bible thus points out that only the "sheep" Gentiles will enter the millennial kingdom, while the "goat" Gentiles will be denied admittance and will be sentenced to eternal punishment. Most of us are Gentiles, and if we fail to be born again now (John 3:3), we could be in the very judgment under discussion, for it is possible for it to take place as soon as seven years from now. You will remember our discussing earlier that the born-again believer will be raptured by Christ before the Tribulation begins (1 Corinthians 15:52; 1 Thessalonians 4:17), then the Tribulation will run for seven years upon the earth (Daniel 9:27), and then this judgment of the living Gentiles will transpire.

You and I will be in one of four positions during this Gentile judgment: (1)Hopefully, we will have gone in the Rapture, lived with Christ in heaven for seven years, and returned with Him to the earth, and will be a spectator at this judgment. (2)Or, we could fail to go in the Rapture, die or be killed as a sinner during the Tribulation, and thus not appear at this judgment, for we would be judged later instead, at the White Throne Judgment after the Millennium. (3)Another possibility is that we could fail to go in the Rapture, and then turn completely to Christ during the Tribulation, then survive that seven-year bloodbath, and be living and appear in this judgment. (4)Finally, we could miss the Rapture, accept Christ during the Tribulation and then die. In that case, we would be resurrected before the Millennium begins.

Speaking of turning to Christ after the Rapture, it may be very difficult for us to turn to Him then, if we constantly and consciously reject Him now before the Rapture. If a person has any intention of ever being converted to the Lord, he should come to Him now. He should not wait, hoping to accept Him during the trying days of the Tribulation.

The First Resurrection

The Bible bears out that the first resurrection will consist of several phases, one being the resurrection just before the Millennium. There are actually five resurrections referred to in the Scriptures: (1)The resurrection of our Lord as the beginning of the first resurrection (1 Corinthians 15:23). (2)Then comes the resurrection at the Rapture of all people who died in Christ during the Church age (1 Thessalonians 4:16). (3)The third phase of the first resurrection will take place when Christ returns to the earth to set up the Millennium, and it will consist of the saved who died during the Tribulation (Revelation 20:- 3-5). (4)Also, many Bible scholars believe that this is when the Old Testament saints will rise (see Daniel 12:2; Isaiah 26:19).

While the first four phases of the first resurrection will involve those who will receive eternal life, the fifth and final resurrection, known as the second resurrection, will be of the unsaved dead and will take place after the Millennium. These millions upon millions of souls who have died outside of God down through the ages will receive eternal damnation at that time (see Revelation 20:5, 11-14).

Satan Will Be Bound

As the way is cleared for Christ's peaceful reign, Satan will be restrained. John wrote: "Then I saw an angel come down from heaven with the key to the bottomless pit and a heavy chain in his hand. He seized the Dragon—that old Serpent, the devil, Satan—and bound him in chains for 1,000 years, and threw him into the bottomless pit, which he then shut and locked, so that he could not fool the nations any more until the thousand years were finished" (Revelation 20:1-3 TLB).

This thousand-year incarceration of Satan will give the earth peace and tranquility such as it has not known since Eden. The Bible identifies Satan as the "god of this age" and "the prince of the power of the air" (Ephesians 2:2), but the day will come when he will be bound and cast into the bottomless pit. Then after being released for a short while at the end of the Millennium, he will be cast into the lake of fire where he will stay throughout eternity.

Pre-, A-, or Post- ?

Before taking a look at the magnificent Millennium, mention should be made here of the three schools of thought about the thousand-year period. You may know that the viewpoints are known as the premillennial, the postmillennial, and the amillennial.

The *postmillenarian* believes that the Church will finally overcome evil, hence the world will become better and better. This world will finally become the Kingdom of God, it is taught, and the Kingdom will last for a thousand years, followed by the return of Christ to the earth. Though this doctrine was quite popular in other years, two world wars, a constant worsening of world conditions, and the decline of Christian influence in world society has caused this position to be less popular than formerly.

The *amillenarian* does not believe that there is to be an earthly Millennium either by man improving himself or by the return of Christ. Rather, he teaches that Christ will continue to convert man to Himself until the world comes to an end. At that time Christ will return and carry out a general resurrection and a general judgment. The judgment will separate the redeemed from the lost. The amillenarian, like the postmillenarian, does not take the prophetic Scriptures literally, but rather applies the so-called spiritual interpretation.

The *premillenarian* knows that at times the Bible speaks in symbols; nonetheless, he believes that the Bible should be taken literally unless it is evident that a passage has another interpretation. In other words, he asks, "If the passage makes sense,

why seek some other sense?" Most of us are premillennialists.
We expect Christ to come in the Rapture, and this event to be
followed by the Tribulation, after which Christ will return to
the earth and set up His thousand-year reign. Since we believe
that Christ must return before the Millennium, we are called
premillennialists.

In summation, then, the postmillenarian believes that Christ
will return after the Millennium; the amillenarian does not
believe that there will be a Millennium; and the premillenarian
believes that Christ will return to the earth before the Millennium.

When Christ Reigns

When Jesus came to this earth, you will recall, He came as
" . . . a Lamb slain from the foundation of the world," but when
He comes the second time, He will not come as a Lamb. The
next time He comes as "the Lion of the tribe of Juda" (Revelation 5:5). This coming will be in power, authority and majesty,
and He will reign in splendor and righteousness. Isaiah describes that reign: " . . .the government shall be upon his shoul-
der: and his name shall be called Wonderful, Counsellor, The
mighty God, The everlasting Father, The Prince of Peace"
(Isaiah 9:6).

Who Will Repopulate the Earth?

Jesus said that immortals will not marry, but will be as angels
(Mark 12:25), therefore the millions of saints who will return
with Christ to the earth and go with Him into the Millennium
will not multiply. The world's increase in population will come
from the people living here upon earth at the beginning of the
Millennium.

Because of the lack of germs and disease, and because of the restoration of Old Testament longevity, the earth will quickly repopulate after the devastating years of the Tribulation. Can you conceive of people again living to be eight or nine hundred years old? It seems that will be the case then. Listen to Isaiah: "There shall be no more thence an infant of days, nor an old man that hath not filled his days: for the child shall die a hundred years old; but the sinner being a hundred years old shall be accursed" (65:20).

If a person is a hundred years old, he will be thought of as a child, while if by the time an individual reaches that age he has not committed himself to the Lord, he "shall be accursed," probably meaning that God will not tolerate his sins beyond that age and he will die.

Apparently, some men will live to be nearly a thousand years old, thus population will grow at an unbelievable rate. By the end of the thousand years, the earth's populace will be "as the sand of the sea" (Revelation 20:8). If you can imagine almost everyone still being alive today who has been born since A.D. 1000, you can get some idea of the world population at the end of the Millennium.

Immortals During the Millennium

Should the Lord Jesus come today and you and I go with Him in the Rapture, we would return with Him as immortals when He comes to rule the world. Our precise function as immortals during the Millennium has been debated by the Church for centuries. Will the immortal mingle freely with the mortal? Will he eat, sleep and be a member of earth's society? In his *Things To Come* Dr. J. Dwight Pentecost states his belief that: "The essential character of and purpose in the millennium leads to the conclusion that resurrected individuals, although having a part in the millennium, are not on the earth to be subjects of the King's reign."

Commenting on the immortals during the Millennium, Dr. Charles C. Ryrie in his book *The Bible and Tomorrow's News,* states: "those who, like the Church, have resurrection bodies, will not be subject to physical limitations. Nor will they contribute to space, food or governmental problems during the Millennium. On the contrary, they will share in Christ's righteous rule."

Government in the Millennium

In His rule of the world, "the Lord shall be King over all the earth: in that day shall there be one Lord, and his name one" (Zechariah 14:9). Jerusalem will be the world capital (Isaiah 2:3), and will be a city of great glory (Isaiah 24:23), and the temple will be located there (Isaiah 33:20). Ruling with perfect justice, Christ " . . . shall not judge after the sight of his eyes, neither reprove after the hearing of his ears: But with righteousness shall he judge the poor, and reprove with equity for the meek of the earth: and he shall smite the earth with the rod of his mouth, and with the breath of his lips shall he slay the wicked. And righteousness shall be the girdle of his loins, and faithfulness the girdle of his reins (Isaiah 11:3-5).

You may not have noticed that the Bible speaks of David's rule in the Millennium (Jeremiah 30:9; Ezekiel 37:24,25). Having been resurrected after the Tribulation along with other Old Testament saints, he will apparently be a regent or prince. Under him nobles and governors will serve (Jeremiah 30:21; Isaiah 32:1). Further, the twelve disciples will rule over the twelve tribes of Israel (Matthew 19:28). Besides these, there will be lesser posts of authority, such as those over ten cities or five cities (Luke 19-28). Also judges will be active, for "I will restore thy judges as at the first, and thy counsellors as at the beginning . . . " (Isaiah 1:26).

Godliness and Righteousness Everywhere

In that day it will be popular to be godly and the ungodly will be very much in the minority. Zechariah speaks of the holiness of the kingdom: "In that day shall there be upon the bells of the horses, HOLINESS UNTO THE LORD; and the pots in the Lord's house shall be like the bowls before the altar. Yea, every pot in Jerusalem and in Judah shall be holiness unto the Lord of hosts . . ." (Zechariah 14:20,21).

You will note in the Scriptures that only the righteous are admitted into the Millennial kingdom (Matthew 25:37). The Messiah, described as ". . .the Sun of righteousness. . .with healing in his wings" (Malachi 4:2) says, "I bring near my righteousness; it shall not be far off" (Isaiah 46:13). Righteousness and peace are the cornerstones of the Millennium, and the people". . .shall dwell in a peaceable habitation, and in sure dwellings, and in quiet resting places" (32:18). In the Millennium, it can be said in fact, "Mercy and truth are met together; righteousness and peace have kissed each other" (Psalms 85:-10).

Of course, a man may sin against God during the Millennium, but mankind's behavior will generally be on a much higher level than now, for Satan will not be there to tempt man. If a person is not genuinely righteous, he will be forced to give outward allegiance to Christ, for the Lord will not condone rebellion then.

The Animal Kingdom Changed

Have you noticed how much the Bible says about the animals in the Millennium? They will not be vicious; apparently they will not be carnivorous; and they will be gentle to the point that a child can have a lion for a pet. Isaiah tells us about it: "The wolf also shall dwell with the lamb, and the leopard shall lie down with the kid; and the calf and the young lion and the fatling together; and a little child shall lead them. And the cow and the bear shall feed. . .and the lion shall eat straw like the ox" (11:6,7). Later, Isaiah talks about the animals again. He says, "The wolf and the lamb shall feed together, and the lion shall eat straw like the bullock. . ." (65:25).

Peace, Wonderful Peace

Today frustrated statesmen grapple with international problems as they faithfully labor to stave off war. Constantly we are beating our plowshares into swords (Joel 3:2) as our defense expenditures drain our treasuries. This will not be so in the Millennium. Then "they shall beat their swords into plowshares, and their spears into pruninghooks: nation shall not lift up a sword against nation, neither shall they learn war any more" (Micah 4:3).

Apparently in Eden, Adam and Eve had no reason to fear the animals, for it seems that they were not vicious before the curse. In the Millennium the curse placed on the earth when Adam sinned will be lifted, except death, and then "Babies will crawl safely among poisonous snakes, and a little child who puts his hand in a nest of deadly adders will pull it out unharmed (Isaiah 11:8 TLB).

Nobody Will Go Hungry

You will find the Bible to be explicit concerning the productivity of the earth during the Millennium. The original curse placed upon the plant and animal kingdom will be lifted and the ground will bring forth bountifully. The seasons will be perfect and ". . .the plowman shall overtake the reaper, and the treader of grapes him that soweth seed" (Amos 9:13). In other words, the crops will be so large that the workers will not be through gathering them before it is time to plant again.

The phenomenon of nature returning to its former glory means that choking weeds and harmful plants will cease to exist, so will the burning deserts (see Isaiah 11; 35; 43). Note the marvelous promises given by Isaiah: "Then the eyes of the blind shall be opened, and the ears of the deaf shall be unstopped. Then shall the lame man leap as an hart, and the tongue of the dumb sing: for in the wilderness shall waters break out, and streams in the desert. And the parched ground shall become a pool, and the thirsty land springs of water . . ." (35:5-7).

Gentiles in the Millennium

In order for Christ's thousand-year reign to encompass the whole world, it must, of course, include the Gentile as well as the Jew. The non-Jew is promised participation in the kingdom, and you will find many passages referring to the fact. Speaking through the prophet Zechariah, Christ said, "And many nations shall be joined to the Lord in that day, and shall be my people: and I will dwell in the midst of thee, and thou shalt know that the Lord of hosts hath sent me unto thee" (3:11).

Like the Jew, the Gentile must be saved to enter the Millennium. Of course, like the Jew, his children will have to be converted. As you can imagine, fifteen or twenty years after the start of the Millennium, there will be many teen-agers who will have been born after the kingdom began. They must be born again individually (Hebrews 11:6; Romans 4:3). However, it will be easy to commit oneself to Christ then, ". . .for the earth shall be full of the knowledge of the Lord, as the waters cover the sea" (Isaiah 11:9). Little wonder that ". . .the sinner being an hundred years old shall be accursed" (Isaiah 65:20).

Presence of the Holy Spirit

Though the Millennium will be an earthly kingdom, its most distinguishing quality will be its spirituality. It will be common for men to be filled with the Spirit. Israel is promised the Spirit: "And I will put my Spirit in you, and ye shall live, and I will place you in your own land. . ." (Ezekiel 37:14).

The Spirit's infilling will be exemplified in worship and praise to the Lord by Jews and Gentiles. Men will willingly obey the Messiah's precepts, for they will possess spiritual power and soul transformation (Isaiah 32:15; Ezekiel 39:29). Apparently the Holy Spirit will be poured out "upon all flesh" for it seems that almost everybody will be Spirit-filled.

In contrast to today's spiritual apathy and worldliness, then there will be spiritual fervor, joyful worship, universal knowledge and understanding of holy truth, and an encompassing fellowship of the saints. Holy living and obedience to God will exist everywhere. Such is the behavior of men filled with the Spirit.

Worship During the Millennium

Much adoration will be given to the Lord Jesus during His thousand-year reign. "And in that day thou shalt say, O Lord,

I will praise thee. . ." Isaiah tells us (12:1). It seems that Isaiah overflows with worship himself as he continues, "Therefore with joy shall ye draw water out of the wells of salvation. And in that day shall ye say, Praise the Lord, call upon his name, declare his doing among the people. . . .Sing unto the Lord . . ." (vs. 3-5).

You will notice that Jeremiah discusses worship also. ". . . the voice of them that shall say, Praise the Lord of hosts: for the Lord is good; for his mercy endureth for ever: and of them that shall bring the sacrifice of praise into the house of the Lord . . ." (33:11). Everybody will worship the Lord then, for Isaiah tells us, "And it shall come to pass. . .shall all flesh come to worship before me, saith the Lord" (66:23).

A magnificent temple will stand in Jerusalem, and Ezekiel describes it and the worship there in minute detail (41:1-25). Though men will praise and worship the Lord throughout the earth, the focal point of worship will be the temple. You will note the discussion of worship, as you read Zechariah 14. Once a year all the nations of the earth "shall even go up from year to year to worship the King, the Lord of hosts, and to keep the feast of tabernacles" (v. 16).

In case a nation, probably through representatives, fails to worship the Messiah at Jerusalem, that nation will be punished by having no rain upon its crops (v. 17). However, almost everyone will gladly worship the Lord. After receiving a new, spiritual heart (Jeremiah 31:33), the forgiveness of sins (v. 34), and the fullness of the Spirit (Joel 2:28,29), people around the world will bow down and worship the incomparable Son of God, the Rose of Sharon, the Prince of Peace.

For the duration of His thousand-year reign, the Rose of Sharon will bloom forth in all of His beauty, purity and magnificence. All the world will bask in the fragrance of His holy rule.

Though the world today is sin-sick and ugly, the Lord Jesus, who is "the rose of Sharon, and the lily of the valleys" (Song of Solomon 2:1), will someday spread righteousness, beauty, and dignity throughout the universe.

Satan Released for Awhile

Like an ugly blight spreading across a beautiful rose garden the spirit of Satan will reach throughout the world at the end of the Millennium. Though his freedom will only last for a short period, Satan will cause thousands of people to rally to him. John tells us, "And when the thousand years are expired, Satan shall be loosed out of his prison" (Revelation 20:7).

This deceiver of man, ever bent on pulling people from God to himself, goes "out to deceive the nations" and "to gather them together to battle" (v. 8). It is astounding that many people will join him and come up against Jerusalem to attack that city (v. 9). You and I may well ask why anybody would turn from the righteous, just rule of Christ to the way of Satan. However, the answer may be obvious.

First, only earthly people ("the nations," v.8) will be involved in this rebellion, not the resurrected saints, who will be immortals throughout the Millennium. The uprising infers that many people will be giving Christ outward allegiance, while their hearts will not be righteous. Christ's rule will be just and fair; nonetheless He will rule with a rod of iron (Revelation 2:27), probably meaning that disobedience will be dealt with summarily. However, when at the end of the Millennium people are given a choice between Satan and Christ, some will turn to Satan.

At the end of His thousand-year reign, it appears that Christ will veil His glory for awhile, and Satan will be permitted to tempt men, thus revealing those who will be giving only feigned obedience to the Lord. As has been pointed out earlier, children will be born throughout the Millennium (Isaiah 11:6,8; Zechariah 8:5), and those people will have to be born again; that is, they will will have to have a spiritual conversion.

You have probably already noticed that the spiritual rebirth will be as essential during the Millennium as it is now. The end-time rebellion clearly points up that fact, demonstrating two things: (1)Man can live in a virtual garden of Eden, yet his need of a personal conversion to Christ still exists. (2)Though one's environment is righteous, just, and holy, if he fails to personally turn to Christ, he is a rebel at heart and may oppose the Lord under temptation.

Rebels Against God Always Lose

You will observe in Revelation 20:8 that apparently hundreds of thousands of people will rebel against God and will ally themselves with Satan. However, compared to the billions upon earth then, the rebellion will probably be small. God will act quickly in putting an end to this sinful rebellion. Fire will rain "down from God out of heaven" (v. 9) and will destroy Satan's army before it strikes.

Then Satan, the chief rebel of the ages, will forever be done away with. Here we come to what may be the major reason that Satan would steer people away from the Book of Revelation, telling them that it is difficult and irrelevant. He wants mankind to believe that he does not even exist, thus giving him free hand to carry on unhindered.

However, God's Holy Word tells us of Satan, and Revelation reveals his utter defeat. He will not finally triumph, but instead he will be brought to complete despair and shame. He will be "cast into the lake of fire and brimstone. . .and shall be tormented day and night for ever and ever" (Revelation 20:10).

Now Satan would rather that I not tell you that. In fact, he would much prefer that the entire world not know his final destiny, and this may be one reason that he steers people away from the Book that tells them about it. You will note that when he is cast into hell, he is not king there, but he himself is "tormented day and night."

Of course, when God destroys the people who allied with Satan at the close of the Millennium, they will die and be punished as are all evil men. With their passing, all unsaved mortals are dead. Other people left on earth are dedicated followers of God and are given immortality; they will dwell in the new heaven and earth throughout eternity.

The Great White Throne Judgment

You may well shudder when you read the somber scriptural account of the judgment of all the unsaved people. The magnitude of the parade of resurrected millions upon millions who never turned to God is staggering. Listen to the awful prediction: "And I saw a great white throne and the one who sat upon it, from whose face the earth and sky fled away, but they found no place to hide. I saw the dead, great and small, standing before God; and the Books were opened, including the Book of Life. And the dead were judged according to the things written in The Books, each according to the deeds he had done" (Revelation 20:11, 12 TLB).

What a sobering scene! This is at "the resurrection of damnation" (John 5:29), of which Jesus spoke, and it is for the dead who "lived not again until the thousand years were finished" (Revelation 20:5). No saved person will stand before the white throne; only those whose names are not "in the Lamb's book of life" (21:27).

If you, I or our loved ones do not accept the Lord now as our Saviour, we will stand before Him then as our righteous Judge. Nobody fails to meet the Son of God, for all must bow before Him now, honoring Him as our Saviour and Lord, or we will meet Him then as our Judge. All who appear at the White Throne Judgment are "cast into the lake of fire" (Revelation 20:15). This judgment is not the same as the Judgment Seat of Christ about which we studied earlier. This sober judgment has to do with all the wicked dead of all ages past.

The New Heaven and Earth

After the rebellion and the judgment of the unsaved, John "saw a new heaven and a new earth: for the first heaven and the first earth were passed away. . ." (Revelation 21:1). The earth will be purified by fire. Peter speaks of that fantastic event: ". . .the heavens shall pass away with a great noise, and the elements shall melt with fervent heat, the earth also and the works that are therein shall be burned up. . . .Nevertheless we, according to his promise, look for new heavens and a new earth, wherein dwelleth righteousness" (2 Peter 3:10,13).

As you have probably read, many Bible scholars believe that Peter is saying that the atmosphere and earth will not be destroyed by God, but renovated, making them new, pure and untainted by sinful man. In his *World Aflame*, Billy Graham comments, "Whatever is not suited for the new life of the new world will be destroyed. This is what some call the end of the world, but the world will never end. It will only be changed into a better world." God has said, "Behold, I make all things new" (Revelation 21:5), and He does this by means of fire.

For Ever and Ever

The Apostle Paul had a vision of heaven and later commented that he saw things unlawful to utter. He did say on another occasion, "Eye hath not seen, nor ear heard, neither have entered into the heart of man, the things which God hath prepared for them that love him" (1 Corinthians 2:9). John gave us a glimpse of life then when he said, "And God shall wipe away all tears from their eyes; and there shall be no more death, neither sorrow, nor crying, neither shall there be any more pain: for the former things are passed away" (Revelation 21:4).

It seems evident that throughout eternity we will be busy thinking and doing and participating on a level that our present finite reasoning cannot at all fathom. I am sure that whatever the great mind of Christ has prepared for you and me will be exciting and satisfying. We will spend our eternity with the Lord in worship, in service, and in companionship. What more could our unworthy hearts ask!

9
Things to Come

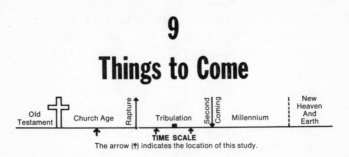

The arrow (↑) indicates the location of this study.

Throughout this book we have studied what the Bible says about things to come. We have delved into prophetic utterances, all of which were made hundreds upon hundreds of years ago. We have been amazed to find that many of those Biblical predictions are being fulfilled during our lifetime.

In fact, more of God's predictive Word has come to fruition during this generation than was fulfilled during the nineteen hundred years between the cross and this age. To many of us it appears evident that the end-time foretold in the Bible, and about which the Church has taught for centuries, is upon us. With these points as a backdrop, I should like to suggest some of the things we can reasonably expect in the days ahead.

1. *Expect Christ to Return.* Though His coming again has been possible for years, never have the times predicted in Scripture been so ripe for His return as today. Therefore expect Him. If you are not ready to go with Him in the Rapture, then get ready immediately. Consider this as a voice crying in the wilderness or as a Paul Revere warning in the night. Christ is coming! Get ready and stay ready for that grand event.

All signs point to the nearness of His coming. The deterioration of morals, the breakdown of law and order, the abrupt increase of violence, the apostasy within the church, and many other developments fulfill scriptural predictions of the end-times.

With all the Christian love and concern that I possess, I ask if you are spiritually prepared to go with Christ in the Rapture. If not, I want to briefly explain how you may give yourself to the Lord Jesus. I call this explanation the Four Absolutes for Eternity.

1. *Repent.* ". . . except ye repent, ye shall all likewise perish" (Luke 13:3). Jesus said these words, and He means for us to have a sorrow for our many sins, and to ask Him to forgive us for them.

2. *Be Reborn.* ". . . Except a man be born again, he cannot see the kingdom of God" (John 3:3). Again, these are the words of Christ and He means them. Call the experience being saved, conversion or whatever, but you cannot be spiritual-minded unless Christ does a work within you which He called being born again.

3. *Believe.* ". . . Believe on the Lord Jesus Christ, and thou shalt be saved . . ." (Acts 16:31). You believe that Christ has saved other people, now believe that He is saving you. It is an act of faith. Believe on Him.

4. *Receive.* ". . . as many as received him, to them gave he power to become the sons of God . . ." (John 1:12). When you receive Christ you become His child. Then you are ready for heaven.

Now continue to pray, read your Bible and witness to your friends about Him. Follow the Lord with all your heart, and you will go in the Rapture.

2. *Expect the Tribulation.* This seven-year period will start immediately after the Rapture of the Church. Then the earth will be even more heartless, violent, and sinful than now. Should Christ come and you fail to go with Him, you may expect to live in those awesome days. It is actually possible for the world to be in that period within a few months from now.

3. *Expect the Common Market.* This European market will probably increase in power and prestige, finally rivaling Russia and the United States. The market may become a deterrent to Russia's political, economic, and ideological advance; that is, if it is in reality the revival of the old Roman Empire.

4. *Expect Middle-East Problems.* Of course, we have them now, but that part of the world will quite probably stay on the front page of the newspapers for a long time. It is there that world interest will ultimately focus.

5. *Expect Morals to Worsen.* Sexual sins are becoming more open and more widespread, and this is a fulfillment of predictive Scripture. Such decadence will probably worsen. Sex acts have been carried out on the stage recently, and homosexuality is a growing menace. It is estimated that in some areas 5 percent of the population is homosexual, meaning that in some single cities with a population of a million, fifty thousand people may be homosexuals.

Sydney Katz, the columnist, forsees women wearing nothing but translucent paint to accentuate their features, with their body covered with a transparent but insulating spray. Sexual debauchery is another sign of the end-times given by the Bible.

6. *Expect Apostasy to Increase.* We have heard the God-is-dead nonsense propounded, and we have seen dancing in the

aisles of the sanctuary after communion. Such apostasized acts will probably increase. In some areas worship has become so godless that people are actually worshiping Satan. Further, we can expect astrology, spiritualism, occultism, and all the rest to increase.

7. *Expect Violence to Continue.* We wonder how this could become much worse. However, as man pulls further and further from God, his inhumanity to his fellow man often increases. It is quite probable that the rate of assaults, riots, and murders will become higher.

8. *Expect Conversions to Continue.* Praise God, all is not dismal ahead! Spiritual revivals such as the Jesus Movement and others will probably continue and spread. People will constantly be converted to Christ as Christians faithfully proclaim the gospel of the Lord Jesus.

9. *Expect Right Living.* Be assured that millions of people are dedicated to the principles of right living laid down in the Bible. Everybody is not going the way of selfish, sensual, sinful living. Many, many people will continue to live upright, godly lives.

10. *Expect Christ to Return.* I repeat this point for emphasis. Christ Himself said He was coming back, and the New Testament writers repeat the theme time and again. Further, these days could well be the very time that He will return. The last words of that magnificent Book, God's Holy Word, read:

He which testifieth these things saith, Surely I come quickly. Amen. Even so, come, Lord Jesus. The grace of our Lord Jesus Christ be with you all. Amen (Revelation 22:20,21).

Bibliography

BOOKS

A Symposium. *The Prophetic Word in Crisis Days.* Grand Rapids: Dunham Publishing Co., 1964.

Babs, James D. *Two Worlds—Christianity and Communism.* Cincinnati: Standard Publishing, 1965.

Benson, David V. *Christianity, Communism and Survival!* Glendale, California: Regal Books, 1967.

Biederwolf, William Edward. *The Millennium Bible.* Grand Rapids: Baker Book House, 1969.

Bjornstad, James, ed. *Twentieth Century Prophecy. Jeane Dixon & Edgar Cayce.* Minneapolis: Bethany Fellowship, Inc., 1969.

Blackstone, W. E. *Jesus Is Coming.* Old Tappan, New Jersey: Fleming H. Revell Co., 1932.

Blair, J. Allen. Living Courageously. Neptune, New Jersey: Loizeaux Brothers, Inc., 1971.

Bloomfield, Arthur E. *A Survey of Bible Prophecy.* Minneapolis: Bethany Fellowship, Inc., 1971.

Bloomfield, Arthur E. *All Things New.* Minneapolis: Bethany Fellowship, Inc., 1967.

Bloomfield, Arthur E. *Signs of His Coming.* Minneapolis: Bethany Fellowship, Inc., 1967.

Bloomfield, Arthur E. *The End of the Days.* Minneapolis: Bethany Fellowship, Inc., 1970.

Britt, George L. *When Dust Shall Sing.* Cleveland, Tennessee: Pathway Press, 1958.

Cox, Clyde C. *Apocalyptic Commentary.* Cleveland, Tennessee: Pathway Press, 1959.

Cox, Clyde C. *Footprints of the Great Tribulation.* Cleveland, Tennessee: Pathway Press, 1961.

Criswell, W. A. *Expository Sermons on the Book of Daniel,* vol. 1. Grand Rapids: Zondervan Publishing House, 1968.
Expository Sermons on Revelation, vol. 2 (1963), vol. 3 (1964), vol. 4 (1965), vol. 5 (1966). Zondervan Publishing House.

Dake, Finis Jennings. *Revelation Expounded.* Tulsa: copyright by author, 1931.

Darms, Anton. *The Jew Returns to Israel.* Grand Rapids: Zondervan Publishing House, 1965.

Davies, J.M. *Israel in Prophecy.* Westchester, Illinois: Good News Publishers, 1967.

DeHaan, M.R. *The Second Coming of Jesus.* Grand Rapids: Zondervan Publishing House, 1944.

DeHaan, M.R. *The Days of Noah.* Grand Rapids: Zondervan Publishing House, 1963.

DeHaan, M.R. *Thirty-five Simple Studies on the Major Themes in Revelation.* Grand Rapids: Zondervan Publishing House, 1971.

DeHaan, Richard M. *Israel and the Nations in Prophecy.* Grand Rapids: Zondervan Publishing House, 1968.

DeKoster, Lester. *Communism and Christian Faith.* Grand Rapids: William B. Eerdmans Publishing Co., 1962.

Drake, H.M. *The Plan of God for the Ages.* Cleveland, Tennessee: Pathway Press, 1966.

Duffield, Guy P. *Tourists' Handbook of Bible Lands.* Glendale, California: Regal Books, 1969.

Duty, Guy. *Christ's Coming and the World Church.* Minneapolis: Bethany Fellowship, Inc., 1971.

Eddleman, H. Leo. *Last Things.* Grand Rapids: Zondervan Publishing House, 1969.

Feinburg, Charles Lee. *Prophecy and the Seventies.* Chicago: Moody Press, 1971.

Ford, W. Herschel. *Simple Sermons on Prophetic Themes.* Grand Rapids: Zondervan Publishing House, 1968.

Goerner, Henry Cornell. *Thus It Is Written.* Nashville: Convention Press, 1959.

Graham, Billy. *World Aflame.* Garden City, New York: Doubleday & Co., Inc., 1965.

Gutzke, Manford George. *Plain Talk on Luke.* Grand Rapids: Zondervan Publishing House, 1966.

Halley, Henry H. *Halley's Bible Handbook.* Grand Rapids: Zondervan Publishing House, 1965.

Howley, G.C.D. *A New Testament Commentary*. Grand Rapids: Zondervan Publishing House, 1969.

Hoyt, Herman A. *The End Times*. Chicago: Moody Press, 1969.

Hughes, Ray H. *The Order of Future Events*. Cleveland, Tennessee: Pathway Press, 1962.

Kac, Arthur W. *The Rebirth of the State of Israel*. Chicago: Moody Press, 1958.

Kirban, Salem. *Guide to Survival*. Wheaton, Illinois: Tyndale House Publishers, 1968.

Kligerman, Aaron J. *Messianic Prophecy in the Old Testament*. Grand Rapids: Zondervan Publishing House, 1957.

Lindsey, Hal. *The Late Great Planet Earth*. Grand Rapids: Zondervan Publishing House, 1971.

Longley, Arthur. *Christ's Return to Rule the World*. Hull, Yorkshire, England. Expositor Publications, 1965.

Lowery, T.L. *Come Quickly, Lord Jesus*. Cleveland, Tennessee: Lowery Publications, 1966.

Lowery, T.L. *The End of the World*. Cleveland, Tennessee: Lowery Publications, 1969.

McMillen, S.I. *Discern These Times*. Old Tappan, New Jersey: Fleming H. Revell Co., 1971.

Mears, Henrietta C. *God's Plan—Past, Present and Future*. Glendale, California: Regal Books, 1971.

Moore, H.L. *The Mark of the Beast*. Franklin Springs, Georgia: n.d.

Munhall, L.W. *The Lord's Return*. Grand Rapids: Kregal Publications, 1962.

Musser, Joe. *Behold A Pale Horse*. Grand Rapids: Zondervan Publishing House, 1970.

Olson, Arnold. *Inside Jerusalem*. Glendale, California: Regal Books, 1968.

Pentecost, J. Dwight. *Things to Come*. Grand Rapids: Zondervan Publishing House, 1964.

Pfeiffer, Charles F. *Jerusalem Through the Ages*. Grand Rapids: Baker Book House, 1967.

Ryrie, Charles C. *The Bible and Tomorrow's News*. Wheaton, Illinois: Scripture Press Publications, Inc., 1969.

Ryrie, Charles Caldwell. *Dispensationalism Today.* Chicago: Moody Press, 1970.

Schwarz, Fred. *You Can Trust the Communist.* Englewood Cliffs, New Jersey: Prentice Hall, Inc., 1960.

Smith, Jim. *Your Incredible Future.* Wheaton, Illinois: Victor Books, 1971.

Smith, Oswald J. *Prophecy—What Lies Ahead?* London: Marshall, Morgan & Scott, 1967.

Smith, Wilbur N. *The Biblical Doctrine of Heaven.* Chicago: Moody Press, 1968.

Smith, Wilbur M. *You Can Know the Future.* Glendale, California: Regal Books, 1971.

Spurgeon, Charles H. *Sermons on the Book of Daniel.* Grand Rapids: Zondervan Publishing House, 1966.

Stedman, Ray C. *What On Earth's Going to Happen?* Glendale, California: Regal Books, 1970.

Stevenson, William. *Strike Zion!* New York: Bantam Books, Inc., 1967.

Strauss, Lehman. *God's Plan for the Future.* Grand Rapids: Zondervan Publishing House, 1965.

Strauss, Lehman. *The End of This Present World.* Grand Rapids: Zondervan Publishing House, 1967.

Strauss, Lehman. *The Prophecies of Daniel.* Neptune, New Jersey: Loizeaux Brothers, 1969.

Synan, J. A. *The Shape of Things to Come.* Franklin Springs, Georgia: Advocate Press, 1969.

Tadford, Frederick A. *The Climax of the Ages.* Grand Rapids: Zondervan Publishing House, 1964.

Tadford, Frederick A. *Lands of the Middle East.* Eastbourne, Sussex, England: Bible and Advent Testimony Movement, n.d.

Talbot, Louis T. *God's Plan of the Ages.* Grand Rapids: William B. Eerdmans Publishing Co., 1946.

Taylor, G.F. *The Second Coming of Jesus.* Franklin Springs, Georgia: Pentecostal Holiness Church, 1950.

Thompson, Fred P., Jr. *Bible Prophecies.* Cincinnati: Standard Publishing, 1964.

Unger, Merrill. *The Haunting of Bishop Pike.* Wheaton, Illinois: Tyndale House Publishers, 1968.

Walvoord, John F. *Daniel, The Key to Prophetic Revelation.* Chicago: Moody Press, 1971.

Walvoord, John F. *The Revelation of Jesus Christ.* Chicago: Moody Press, 1966.

White, John Wesley. *Re-entry.* Grand Rapids: Zondervan Publishing House, 1970.

Whitney, Forrest. *Antichrist on Trial.* Litchfield, Maine: Living Word Press, n.d.

Wood, Leon. *A Survey of Israel's History.* Grand Rapids: Zondervan Publishing House, 1970.

PERIODICALS

"Britain's Mart Vote Big Step for United Europe," *Mobile Press,* October 29, 1971, p. 7-A.

"Business Around the World," *U.S. News & World Report,* November 29, 1971, p. 75

"From the Editor," *Christian Life,* August, 1971, p. 8.

"Jesus Saves: Our Alienated Youth," *Eternity,* August, 1971, p. 8.

"Key to Future World Events," *Moody Monthly,* April, 1965, p. 51.

"The Campus Life Forum," *Campus Life,* August/September, 1971, p. 5.

"The Restoration of David's Tabernacle," *The Church of God Evangel,* August 23, 1971, p. 13.

"What About the Arabs in Israel?" *Lighted Pathway,* July, 1970, p. 12.

"Yesterday, Today, and Forever," *Decision,* May, 1971, p. 12.

Scripture Index